WITHDRAWN

03 MAY 2012

17/10/18

PERTH &
KINROSS
COUNCIL

Education &
Children's Services

thelibrary
don't be lost for words

Tel 01738 444949 • www.pkc.gov.uk/library

Please return/renew this item by the
last date shown
Items may also be renewed by phone or internet

WITHDRAWN

Button Jewellery

Over 25 original designs for necklaces,
earrings, bracelets and more

Sara Withers

D&C
David and Charles

739.27

A DAVID & CHARLES BOOK

David & Charles is an F+W Publications, Inc.
  company
4700 East Galbraith Road
Cincinnati, OH 45236

First published in the UK in 2006

Copyright © 2006 by Breslich & Foss Ltd

Text by **Sara Withers**
Photography by **Lindsey Stock** and
  Martin Norris
Illustrations by **Kuo Kang Chen**
Design by **Elizabeth Healey**
Project management by **Janet Ravenscroft**

Sara Withers has asserted her right to be
identified as the author of this work in
accordance with the Copyright, Designs and
Patents Act, 1988.

All rights reserved. No part of this publication
may be reproduced, stored in a retrieval
system, or transmitted, in any form or by any
means, electronic or mechanical, by
photocopying, recording or otherwise,
without prior permission in writing from the
publisher.

A catalogue record for this book is available
from the British Library.

ISBN-13: 978-0-7153-2579-7 paperback
ISBN-10: 0-7153-2579-5 paperback

Printed in Thailand
for David & Charles
Brunel House   Newton Abbot Devon

Visit our website at
www.davidandcharles.co.uk

David & Charles books are available from all
good bookshops; alternatively you can
contact our Orderline on 0870 9908222 or
write to us at FREEPOST EX2 110, D&C
Direct, Newton Abbot, TQ12 4ZZ (no stamp
required UK only); US customers call 800-
289-0963 and Canadian customers call 800-
840-5220.

Contents

Introduction

Many of you will be experienced in making jewellery and, although there is a fantastic selection of beads on the market, it is always fun to combine them with other objects. Buttons are ideal companions for beads: they come in interesting materials, such as wood and shell, a whole spectrum of glass and a huge selection of plastics. This abundance provides the ideal opportunity to create truly unique pieces of jewellery.

Most of the projects in *Button Jewellery* can be made with buttons other than the ones shown, and we have incuded variations to give you some ideas. Our aim is to inspire you to hunt out exciting buttons to combine with beads. Those of you who enjoy making your own beads can make your own buttons, too.

Some designs require basic tools, while others call for nothing more than a needle. All the tools you need (such as crimping pliers or wire cutters) are specified at the beginning of each project, and are readily available from bead or jewellery suppliers. The wiring and knotting techniques used in the book are shown in the techniques section on pages 120–27.

We hope you will be inspired by gorgeous buttons and have fun making the pieces. Be inventive, and no one else in the world will have exactly the same jewellery as you!

CHAPTER ONE

Necklaces and Chokers

Fashion magazines and jewellery stores are overflowing with wonderful necklaces using masses of shell buttons – just like Pretty Pearls on page 10. Now is your opportunity to make necklaces like these and many other luscious designs.

In this section you will find individual buttons used as a glamorous Crystal Pendant (page 26), and groups of buttons wired together to make a Sparkle Choker (page 42). Some of the designs, such as Fancy Fish (page 46), are very simple; others use more complex wiring and you should practise the techniques before you start.

Pretty Pearls

This design demonstrates how a stunning piece of jewellery can be created with just a few buttons. Pretty mother-of-pearl buttons are wired together with a handful of freshwater pearls and silver beads to form the main section of the necklace and then attached to a suede ribbon so that you can easily adjust the length of the finished piece. Wireworking does require some practice, but is very rewarding because it opens up a whole area of jewellery-making. If you wish, you can create this design with different materials: all you need are a few distinctive two-hole buttons and a selection of small beads. Imagine this necklace made from big glass buttons with crystal beads between them. A suede ribbon adds a special finish, but other materials can be just as effective.

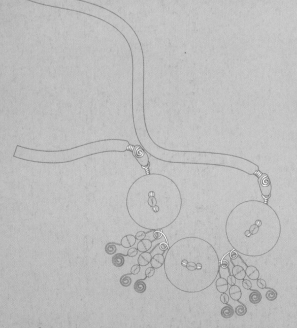

materials

3 two-hole buttons
11 tiny silver beads
8 small freshwater pearls
45cm (18in) 0.6mm silver-plated wire
40cm (16in) 0.4mm silver-plated wire
45–50cm (18–20in) pink suede ribbon, or enough to fit around your neck

tools

wire cutters
round nose pliers
snipe nose pliers

techniques

closed loops, page 123
single coils, page 122

1 Cut 25cm (10in) of the 0.6mm silver-plated wire. Thread the wire through one hole in the first button. Slide a silver bead onto the wire, then bend the wire in the middle and thread it through the remaining button hole.

2 Pull the wire all the way through, then bend it so that the button lies flat on the wire. Run your fingers over the wire a few times to smooth it against the back of the button.

3 Place the round nose pliers around one end of the wire next to the button. Wind the wire around the nose of the pliers to create a small loop.

4 Move the pliers along the wire so that they sit beside the small loop. Wind the wire around the nose to create a second loop. Repeat Steps 3 and 4 on the other side of the button.

5 Thread the second button onto the wire next to the two loops, adding a silver bead between the two button holes as before. Use snipe nose pliers to pull the wire through to the other side of the button, then smooth the wire firmly against the back of the button. Repeat Step 5 to add a third button on the other side of the first button.

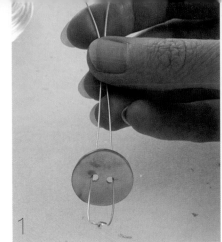

1

2

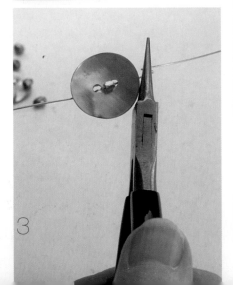

3

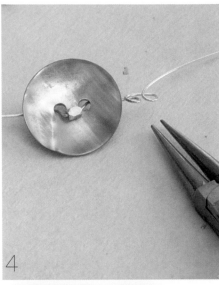

4

5

6 Gently bend the section of buttons to form a slightly bowed shape, with the central button a little forward and below the other two. Make a closed loop in the wire at each end of the button section.

7 Cut two 10cm (4in) pieces of 0.6mm silver-plated wire. Make a small single coil at one end of each wire, then wind the wire around the pliers above the coil to create a small loop at right angles to the coil. Cut the suede ribbon in half. Thread one piece through each closed loop on the main button section so that 2.5cm (1in) of ribbon emerges through each loop.

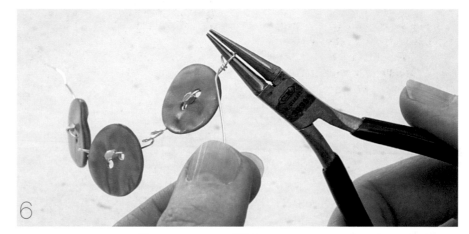

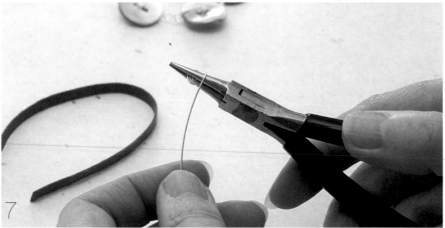

8 Thread each piece of ribbon through one of the new pieces of wire so that the coil sits just above the closed loop. Wind the wire firmly around the ends of the ribbon to hold them in place. Once they are secure, clip off the end of the wire and press it into the ribbon with snipe nose pliers.

9 To decorate the centre of the necklace, cut four 10cm (4in) pieces of 0.4mm silver-plated wire and make a coil at one end of each piece. Thread a pearl and silver bead onto each wire.

10 Work one wire through each of the loops between the buttons. Bend each wire back down at the other side, then thread on a silver bead and pearl. Form a single coil at this end of each wire to secure the beads.

These delicate matching earrings, and those opposite, are made using the same method as the Ocean Earrings on page 102.

VARIATION This striking necklace is made in exactly the same way as the pearl necklace, but the darker shell buttons and black cotton thong create a completely different look. To make the matching earrings, shape the small coils decorated with pearls in the same way as you did in Steps 9 and 10 of the main project, hanging them through one hole in the buttons. The earrings are suspended from earwires with a length of wire through the second hole, using the Wiring to Hang technique (see page 125).

Shell Cluster

materials
26 two-hole shell buttons in
 various shapes
1 larger two-hole button
6m (20ft) strong linen or
 polyester thread

tools
scissors
adhesive tape (optional)
strong needle

techniques
overhand knot, page 126
square knot, page 127

This project involves a lot of knotting, so it requires a degree of patience, but the results are well worth the effort. You will end up with a wonderful cluster of shell buttons that you can wear with many different outfits and will have mastered some basic knotting techniques in the process. The necklace is formed from four strands of buttons, with decorative square knotting at each end. You can easily adjust the length of the necklace by working shorter or longer lengths of knotting. Try to find a selection of buttons in different shapes and alternate them along each strand; oval, square and hexagonal buttons are used here. Although these buttons are in toning natural shades, you could choose from a wider palette of colours if you prefer, and select an appropriate colour thread.

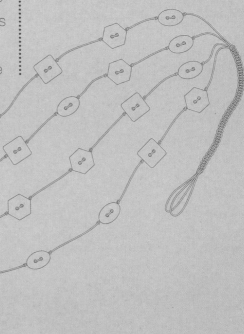

1 Cut the thread into six equal lengths. Set aside two lengths of thread and the larger button. Knot the rest of the buttons onto the four remaining threads, working outward from the centre of each thread. Start by threading a button onto the centre of one of the threads, then make an overhand knot on one side of the button. Place a needle into the knot and use the needle to draw the knot towards the button. Pull the end of the thread to tighten the knot as you position it next to the button.

2 Make another knot on the other side of the button in the same way, then tie a third knot a small distance along the thread where you want to position the next button. Here, the buttons are placed 3–4cm (1¼–1½in) apart.

3 Thread on another button and tie a knot on the other side of it. The knots should sit either side of each button to hold the buttons in place. Continue to work along both ends of the thread until you have a selection of seven buttons spaced out on the thread.

4 Repeat this process on the second thread, but position the buttons so that they align with the spaces between the buttons on the first thread. The completed second thread should have six buttons on it.

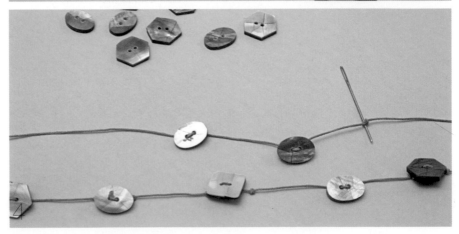

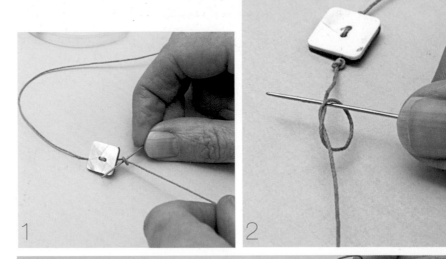
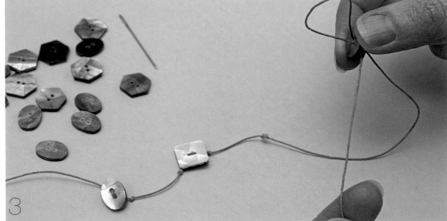

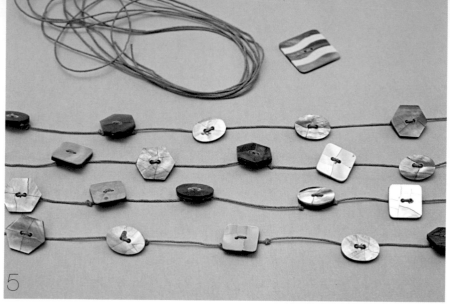

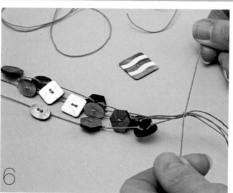

5 Thread another two lengths of thread with buttons in the same way, with seven buttons on the third thread and six buttons on the fourth. Lay out all four threads and check that you are happy with how they look, making adjustments to the positions of the knots and buttons if necessary.

6 Using the two threads you set aside at the beginning, tie one around each end of the button threads, about 5cm (2in) from the buttons.

7 At each end of the necklace, knot one of the button threads to the new thread so that the new thread will not slip out of place.

8 Work each end thread in square knots around the button threads, pulling the button threads straight as you do so. It will help if you secure the other end of the necklace to the worktop with tape while knotting. Continue knotting, working away from the buttons, until you reach about 3cm (1¼in) from the length of necklace you wish to make.

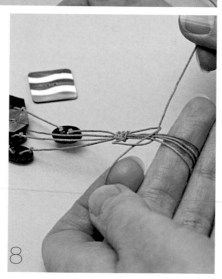

9 At one end of the necklace, thread the large button onto one of the button threads, then fold this thread back towards the knotting.

10 Continue to knot towards the button, taking the knotting as close to the button as possible. Trim the loose ends of thread close to the button.

11 At the other end of the necklace, fold back two of the button threads to form a loop. Trim the remaining two button threads, then knot around both the trimmed and folded button threads until the loop is the correct size to fit around the large button.

12 Work any excess knotting threads back into the knotting with your needle. Trim off any other stray lengths of thread with the scissors.

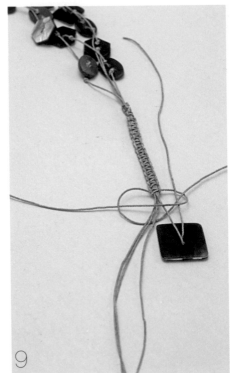

9

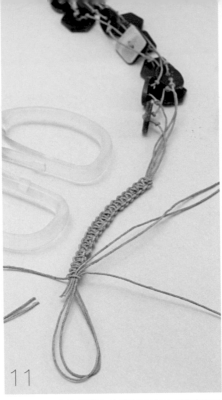

11

10

12

VARIATION The pretty shell buttons used for the main project are all in shades of cream and beige, allowing the natural sheen of the material to become the focus of the piece as the buttons catch the light. However, you could use any buttons you like to make this necklace. Plastic buttons are inexpensive and available in many different colours. Here, vivid primary colours have been chosen to create a funky modern necklace that will look great with streetwear and grab everyone's attention.

materials

1 four-hole button
approx 65 x 3mm silver-plated
balls
20 x 4mm and 5mm crystal beads
approx 20 x 4mm and 6mm
AB-coated round beads
2 x 8mm miracle beads
approx 50 x 7/0 and 8/0 dark
beads
2.6m (9ft) strong polyester thread
T-bar fastener
4 French crimps

tools

scissors
crimping pliers
strong needle

techniques

crimping, page 126
overhand knot, page 126

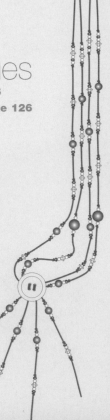

Midnight Blue

This lush mixture of beads and crystals is gathered at the front into a toning button, with strands of beaded thread dangling below the button to form a pleasing shape. Decide on the order you want to thread the beads to ensure you achieve a pleasing, symmetrical design. The kinds of beads used in our necklace are listed, but your choice of beads can be dictated by the central button, or simply use whatever beads you have at hand. AB-coated beads have an aurora borealis coating that produces an iridescent rainbow effect. Miracle beads, also known as wonder beads, have a reflective mirror coating inside, topped with several layers of lacquer. Light passes through the lacquer and is then reflected back to give the beads great shine and depth.

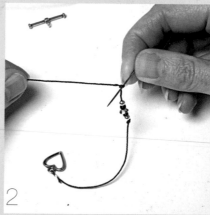

1 Cut the thread into four equal lengths. Thread a French crimp onto the end of one length of thread, then pass the thread through one section of the fastener and back through the crimp. Squeeze the crimp with crimping pliers, then trim the thread.

2 Make an overhand knot in the thread about 5–6cm (2–2½in) from the fastener. Thread on the first group of beads. Tie a knot on the other side of the beads and use the needle to draw the knot close to the beads, pulling the end of the thread to tighten the knot as you move it.

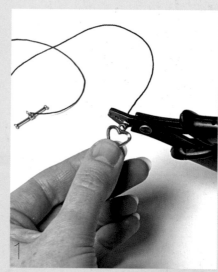

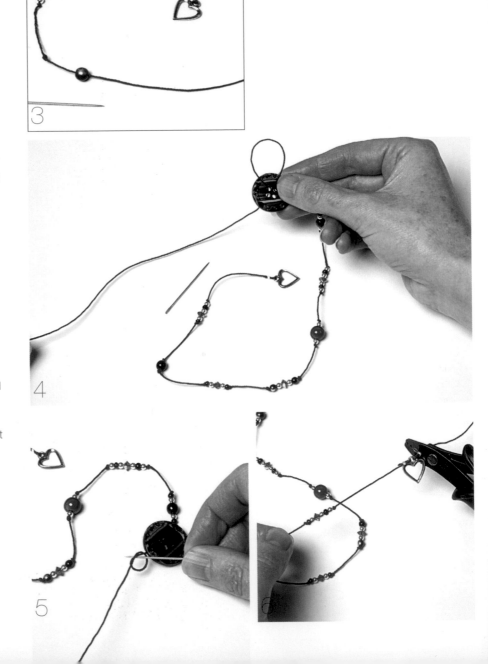

3 Leave a gap of about 3cm (1¼in), then make another knot and thread on another group of beads or a miracle bead, making another knot on the other side as before. Work down the thread in this way, adding groups of beads with knots on either side to hold them in position, until you reach the length where you wish to place the button.

4 Thread on the button from beneath, using an adjacent pair of holes in the button. Push the button up the thread to reach the last group of beads.

5 Make another knot on the side of the button, then add another group of beads. The button should be positioned close enough to the two groups of beads on either side so that it does not move too much, but not so tightly that it gets pushed forwards by the beads. Add one or two more groups of beads to the end of the thread.

6 Crimp a second thread to the heart section of the fastener. Add groups of beads to this thread, positioning them so that they sit between the groups of beads on the first thread.

7 Work this thread through the same button holes as before, then add groups of beads below the button again.

8 Crimp a third thread onto the bar side of the fastener. Copy the groups of beads you made on the first strand, then work the new strand through the remaining pair of holes in the button. Finish the thread with groups of beads below it.

9 Crimp the fourth and final thread onto the bar side of the fastener and add groups of beads to match the second strand. Thread it through the same holes in the button as the third strand, then finish with more groups of beads. When you have completed all four strands, trim the threads that dangle below the button if necessary.

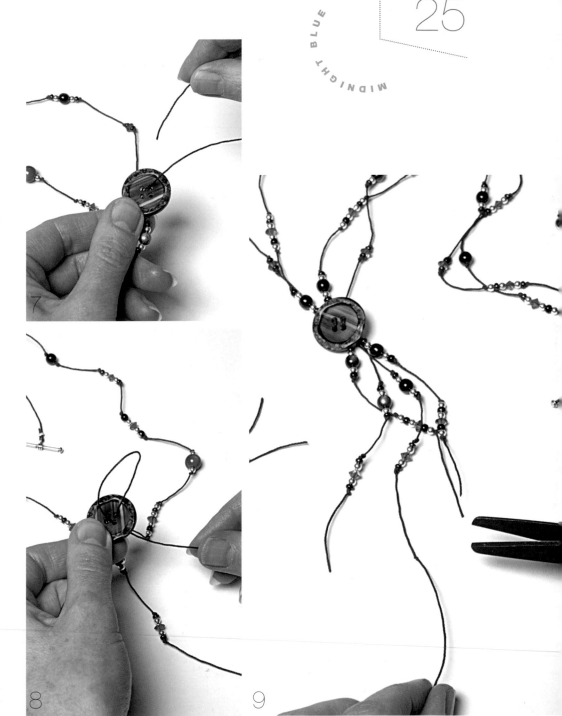

Crystal Pendant

This cluster of dangling Swarovski crystal beads, wired with little coils and loops from an ornate button, create a glorious pendant that you can suspend from a variety of materials. A lilac suede ribbon has been used here, but you could choose a chain or torque if you prefer. The striking button featured in our design is made from shell and has an intricate design etched into its surface. Each of the wires that dangles below the button is embellished with beads in a different order. A selection of silver beads was chosen because these would not detract attention from the button or crystals, but would provide texture and sparkle to the finished pendant.

materials

1 ornate two-hole button
7 x 5mm crystal beads
4 x 4mm crystal beads
21 x 2mm silver-plated balls
2 x 3mm silver-plated balls
6 x 8/0 silver glass beads
90cm (3ft) 0.6mm silver-plated
  wire
suede ribbon to fit around neck
  at desired length

tools

wire cutters
round nose pliers
snipe nose pliers

techniques

single coils, page 122
closed loops, page 123
double coils, page 123
wiring to hang, page 125

1 Cut seven 8cm (3¼in) lengths, one 10cm (4in) length and two 12cm (4¾in) lengths of wire. Make a single coil at one end of a 8cm (3¼in) length of wire using round nose pliers.

2 Set aside two 5mm crystal beads, then thread four or five of the remaining beads onto the wire above the coil. Fix the beads in place with a closed loop.

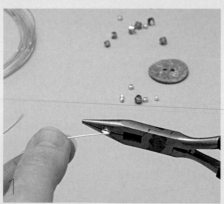

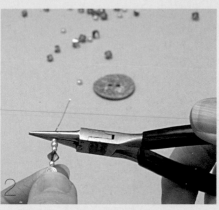

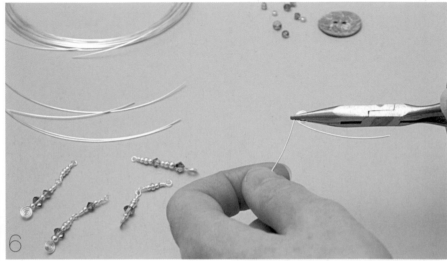

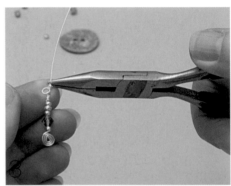

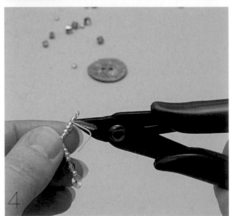

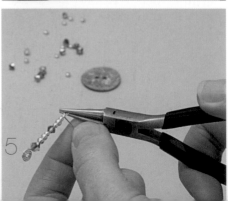

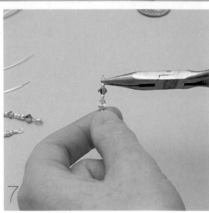

3 Thread the end of another 8cm (3¼in) length of wire through the loop of the first section, then wrap the end of the new wire around to form another closed loop.

4 Thread three beads onto the second section of wire, then form a closed loop at the end. As with all closed loops, use wire cutters to snip off the excess wire, then use snipe nose pliers to press the sharp end back into the wrapped wire below the loop. You have completed the first 'dangle' of the necklace.

5 Make two more dangles in the same way, but with different arrangements of beads. Make the fourth dangle without a central link, starting with a coil and finishing with a closed loop.

6 Make the last dangle using the 10cm (4in) length of wire. Fold it in half and coil up both pieces of wire to form a double coil in the centre.

7 Thread some beads on either side of the coil, then complete the section with a closed loop at each end.

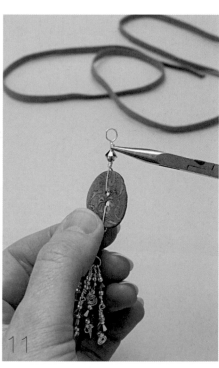

9 Add a 5mm crystal bead above the loop, then thread the long end of the wire through one hole in the button. Fold the end of the wire down the other side of the button. Position the fold so that there is space to wrap the folded wire around the main stem of wire between the button and the crystal bead without losing movement in the whole piece. Trim the wire and press in the sharp end as before.

10 Thread the final 12cm (4³/4in) length of wire through the other hole in the button. Fold the wire about 4cm (1¹/2in) along and wrap the short end around the longer end using the wiring to hang technique.

11 Thread on the remaining 5mm crystal bead, then finish the hanging wire with a final closed loop. Make sure that this loop is large enough for the ribbon or chain to pass through, which you are now ready to add.

8 Take one of the 12cm (4³/4in) lengths of wire and make a large loop around the round nose pliers about 2cm (³/4in) from one end. Thread the dangles onto the loop, then wrap the short end of the wire around the longer end to fix them in place, using the same technique as when creating a closed loop.

materials

14 small two-hole buttons
1 large two-hole button
12 star beads
6 x 3mm crystal beads
24 x 2mm silver-plated balls
110 x 8/0 pearl beads
1.2m (4ft) fine polyester thread
1 barrel fastener
4 French crimps

tools

'Big Eye' or very fine needle
crimping pliers
scissors

techniques

crimping, page 126

Pastel Stars

Delicately coloured buttons are accessorized with tiny pearl beads, stars and crystals to form a light and summery necklace. All of the beads and buttons are in pastel shades, but you could choose a stronger colour theme if you prefer. The star beads complement the decoration of silver stars on the buttons, creating a theme for the necklace. If the buttons you select have a different style of decoration, try to find a bead design that will complement them. A 'Big Eye' needle is formed from two long pieces of metal joined together at the ends, so that the centre of the needle is essentially one big eye. It is therefore very easy to thread, while still being slender enough to pass through small beads.

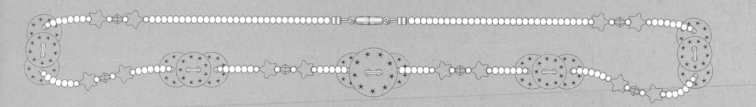

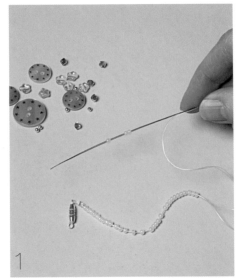

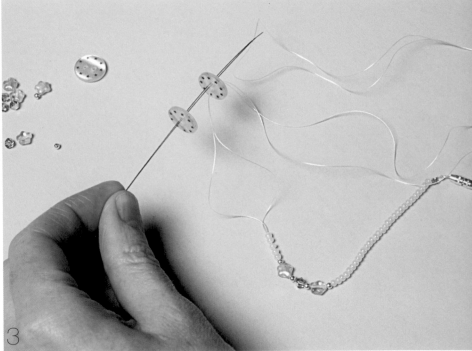

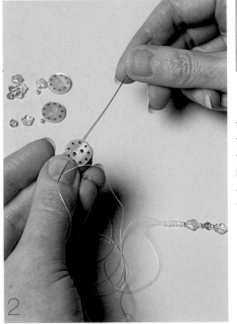

1 Thread the needle, doubling over the threads. Slide two French crimps onto the ends of the thread. Pass the threads through one end of the fastener, then back through the crimps. Squeeze the crimps with crimping pliers, then trim the thread. Thread on 30 pearl beads.

2 Thread on the first group of larger beads, comprising two stars with a crystal between them, with silver-plated balls before and after each bead. Add five more pearl beads, then add the first small button by threading the needle through one of the holes from the front.

3 Bring the needle up through the other hole in the button, then straight through one of the holes in the second small button, threading from the back.

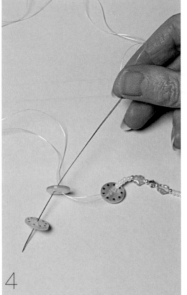

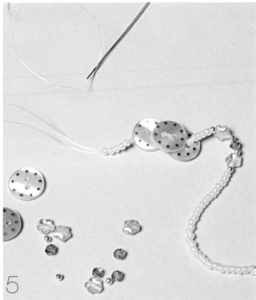

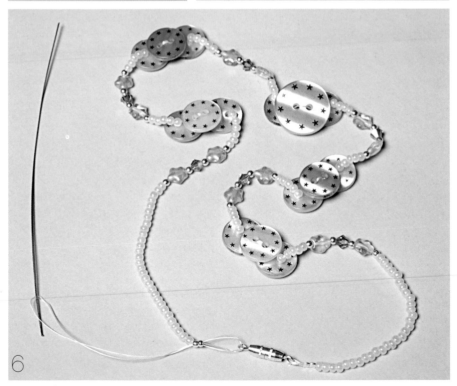

4 Take the thread back through the other hole in the second button, then straight through one of the holes in the third small button, threading from the front.

5 Bring the thread back up through the other hole in the third button. Check that all the buttons are facing upwards, then thread on another five pearl beads.

6 Follow these with another group of star and crystal beads, then five more pearl beads and another group of three buttons. Continue in this way, adding groups of beads and buttons interspersed with pearl beads. When you add the third group of buttons, place the larger button in the centre. When you have threaded on the last group of star and crystal beads, add 30 more pearl buttons so that the design is symmetrical. Finish the necklace by crimping the thread to the other end of the fastener.

Black Beauty

This simple but effective choker is very easy to make. The buttons are threaded in the same way as the Big Buttons bracelet on page 74, but the choker is finished with lengths of half-knotting to make it long enough to wear around the neck. The buttons will sit better against the neck if you keep the choker fairly short. We used black thread to complement the black base colour of the buttons, but you should choose a colour of thread that suits the buttons you are using. All of the buttons in this design are the same, but you could alternate buttons in two or three different designs, or even use 15 completely different buttons. When purchasing the buttons for the choker, remember to buy extra if you want to make a matching big button bracelet.

materials
15 two-hole buttons
3m (10ft) strong, thick black thread
2 spring ends
1 hook

tools
scissors
snipe or flat nose pliers
adhesive tape (optional)

techniques
half knot, page 127

1 Cut the thread into one 60cm (2ft) length and two 1.2m (4ft) lengths. Use the shorter length to thread the buttons. It is easiest to start with a central button, so pass an end of thread through each hole in the button from the front. Make sure that the button is in the centre of the thread.

2 Add buttons on either side of the central one, threading up through one hole and down through the other hole in each button. Adjust the tension of the thread as you work so that the buttons overlap each other slightly. The buttons will not stay in place all the time, but you will be able to adjust them easily.

3 When all of the buttons have been threaded, use the two remaining longer threads to work a length of half knots at each end of the button thread. Start by tying one of the longer lengths around one end of the button thread, sliding the knot into position under the buttons.

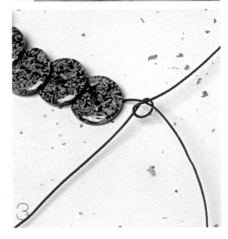

4 Knot the button thread to one end of the new thread so that the new thread will not slip out of place.

5 Work the new thread in half knots around the button thread, pulling the button thread straight as you do so. It will help if you secure the other end of the choker to the worktop with tape while knotting. Continue knotting, working away from the buttons, until you reach about 3cm (1¼in) from the length of choker you wish to make. Work a length of half knots at the other end of the choker in the same way.

6 At one end of the choker, work the threads through a spring end and use snipe or flat nose pliers to squeeze the last row of the spring into the threads. When the spring end is secure, cut off the ends of threads as close to the spring end as possible.

7 Attach a spring end to the other end of the choker. Use pliers to twist open the loop on the hook, making sure that you open the loop sidewise so that you do not weaken the metal. Slip the loop through the top of the spring end, then twist the loop closed again.

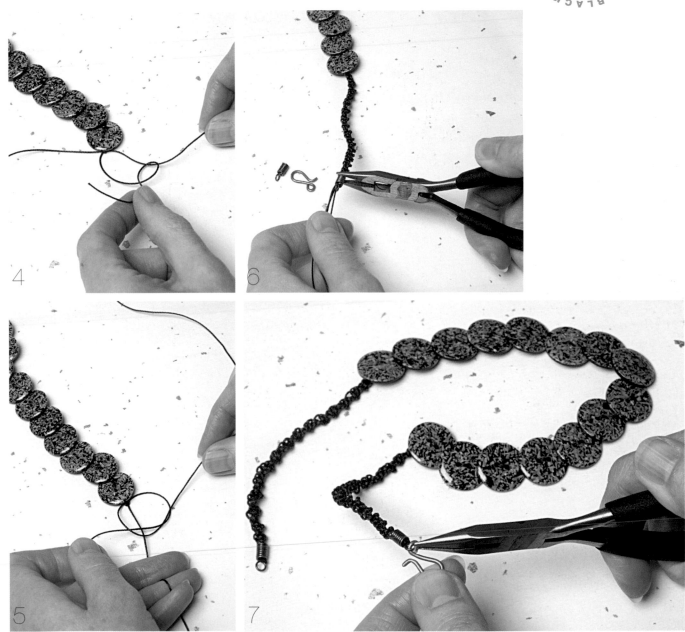

4

5

6

7

materials

5 two-hole heart buttons
6 dichroic tube beads
1.4m (5ft) strong polyester thread
1 barrel fastener
2 French crimps

tools

scissors
strong needle
crimping pliers

techniques

overhand knot, page 126
crimping, page 126

Hearts Galore

This bright knotted necklace is ideal for a child to wear, or anyone who is young at heart. You do not have to spend a lot of money on buttons to make attractive jewellery. These plastic multicoloured heart-shaped buttons, when combined with a strong thread and a few bright dichroic glass tube beads, create a cheerful effect. However, you could select a more elegant button design to achieve a glamorous result. The length of thread suggested here will make quite a short necklace, but you can make a longer one if you prefer. If you do make a longer necklace, space the buttons and beads as shown here, leaving the ends of thread unadorned or decorated with a few extra knots.

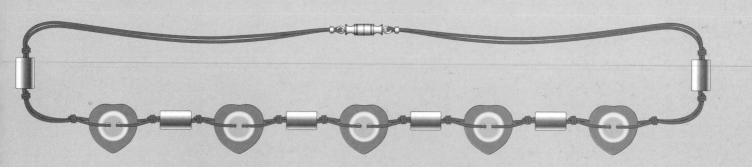

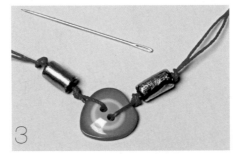

1 Cut the thread in half and start forming the necklace from the centre outwards. Pass one of the threads halfway through one of the holes in the first button. Hold both ends of the thread together and make an overhand knot. Place the needle into the knot and draw it close to the button, pulling the ends of the thread to tighten the knot as you do so. Make sure that the ends of the thread are even and that the button is lying flat. Repeat with the second length of the thread in the remaining button hole.

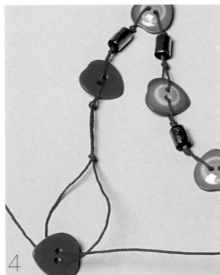

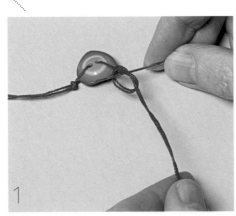

2 On one side of the button, work both ends of the thread through a dichroic tube bead. Tie a knot on the other side of the tube bead as you did in Step 1.

3 Thread a dichroic tube bead onto the other side of the central button and secure it in place with a knot.

4 Work up both sides of the necklace, alternating buttons and beads and spacing them with knots. To add each button, pass a thread down through the first hole and the other thread up through the second hole. Space the beads and buttons to suit the length of your design, creating larger gaps if you want the necklace to be a little longer.

5 When you have reached the required length, make sure that the beads and buttons are sitting together well. Finish the necklace by attaching the threads to each end of the fastener with French crimps, then trim off any loose ends.

VARIATION This necklace is made in exactly the same way as the heart necklace, but uses a different colour scheme and button design to create a dramatically different effect. The buttons are made from transparent plastic embedded with silver glitter, and these are complemented by silver dichroic tube beads. The beads and buttons are knotted together with black thread to create a sparkling monochromatic necklace that would work perfectly with any party outfit.

Sparkle Choker

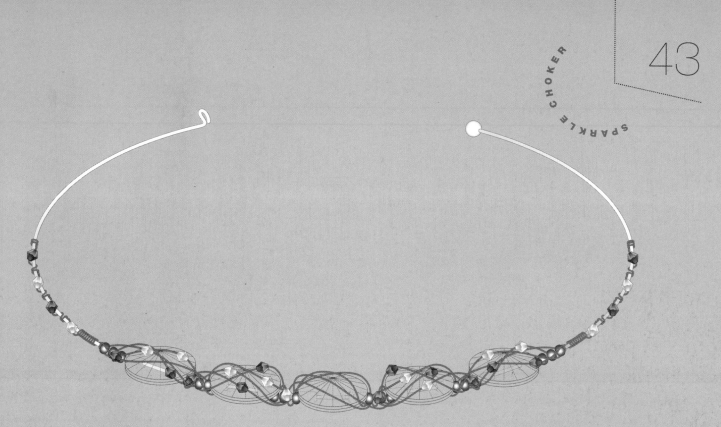

This glamorous piece of jewellery is great fun both to make and to wear. Although you can re-create the choker demonstrated here exactly, the design of the piece provides a great chance to add your own personal touch, by deciding how much wire you want to wrap around the buttons and how many crystals to add. You will probably want to do a lot of wrapping because it is so much fun. The faceted buttons are complemented by faceted crystals, so that the choker catches and bounces light around from all angles. Choose round beads and coloured wire in toning shades to the buttons and crystals so that nothing detracts from the sparkling light. Use heavy-duty wire cutters to cut the torque because the wire will be too strong for a more delicate pair and could damage them.

materials

5 buttons with a hole through the back
30–40 x 3mm crystal beads
18 x 6/0 round beads
1 silver or silver-plated torque, slightly larger than your neck size
1.5–2m (5–7ft) 0.6mm coloured wire

tools

large wire cutters
snipe nose pliers
round nose pliers
file

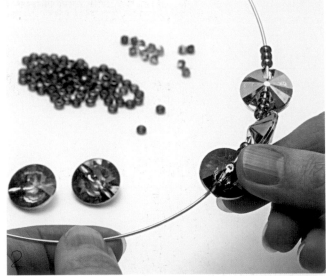

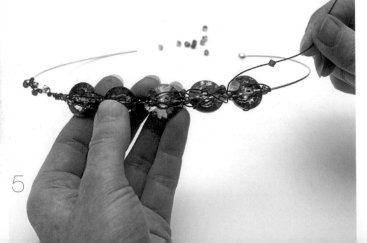

1 Most torques are manufactured with a ball at one end and a curl of wire at the other end. Start by clipping off the curled end with wire cutters.

2 Thread on the buttons and round beads, arranging them as you like. Here, the buttons are quite close together, with three round beads before and after each button.

3 Now the fun begins. Wind the coloured wire firmly around one end of the torque about 8cm (3in) from the end and smooth in the end of the wire with snipe nose pliers. Continue wrapping the wire around the torque, adding crystals as you work. Make it as regular or random as you like.

4 When you reach the beads and buttons, wrap the wire over these as well. Make sure that you position the button section slightly off-centre. When you finish the choker, you will have to remake the loop that you cut off the torque in Step 1, so you need slightly more length on this side. Work over each button and between them, adding crystals as you go. Push the buttons together and make them face forwards.

5 When you reach the other side of the button section, turn around and work back across the buttons, wrapping the wire and adding more crystals as before. Repeat this several times until you achieve the look that you like. Crisscross the wire and push everything into shape as you work.

6 To recreate our rich look, wrap four times across the button section. This means that the wrapping wire will end up at the first side of the torque, so you will need to clip off the wire here and smooth in the end.

7 Attach the wire on the other side of the button section as you did in Step 3. Continue wrapping and adding crystals to match the first side of the torque.

8 To finish, use round nose pliers to bend the torque at a 90-degree angle about 1cm (³⁄₈ in) from the end. Curve this end of wire around to form a loop that will clip around the ball at the other end of the torque to fasten it. You may need to file the end to make it smooth.

materials
3 two-hole fish buttons
16 magatama beads
1–1.1m (3–3¹/₂ft) nylon
monofilament
24 tiny French crimps
2 larger French crimps
1 T-bar fastener

tools
scissors
crimping pliers

techniques
crimping, page 126

Fancy Fish

This is a bright and cheerful way to use a few quirky buttons. Although frosted fish buttons have been used here, you could use any style of button that you like. When selecting beads, choose ones that will complement the buttons as well as the clear glass magatama beads used here do. These teardrop-shaped beads with off-centre holes work perfectly next to the fish buttons because they look like tiny bubbles. If you want to make a longer necklace, simply use longer pieces of monofilament, and add more magatama beads and perhaps more buttons. We chose a classic T-bar fastener to complete the necklace, but you could use another style if you prefer. Bear in mind that a simple clasp suits the mood of this choker better than a more elaborate one.

1

1 Cut the monofilament in half and thread the central fish button onto the middle of both pieces by passing one thread up through one button hole, and the other thread down through the other button hole. Holding the ends of one thread together at the side of the button, work them through one of the tiny crimps and squeeze them with crimping pliers. Crimp the second thread on the other side of the button.

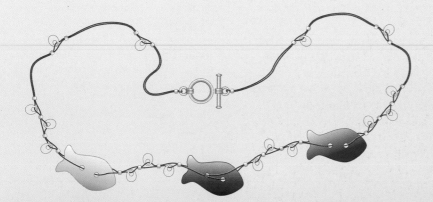

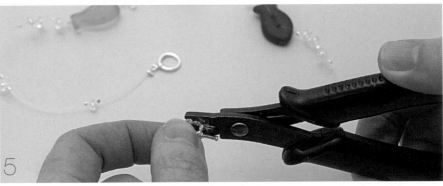

2 On one side of the button, thread a magatama bead onto one strand of thread, then add a tiny crimp to hold the two strands together again. Add two more magatama beads and crimps on this side of the button, positioning the beads on alternating strands. Repeat this process to add three magatama beads on the other side of the button.

3 Add another fish button, threading one strand down through one button hole and the other strand up through the other button hole. Secure the bead with a crimp at the other side. Add three more magatama beads after this button, and thread on another fish button and group of magatama beads on the other side of the choker, interspersed with crimps.

4 Decorate the rest of the thread by adding a few more of the magatama beads between the strands, holding them in place with tiny crimps.

5 Finish by threading both strands at one end of the choker through one of the larger crimps, then through one section of the fastener and back through the crimp. Squeeze the crimp with crimping pliers, then repeat to join the remaining section of the fastener to the other end of the choker. Cut off any excess thread on both sides.

VARIATION If a brightly coloured fish choker is not to your taste, you can easily adapt the design to create a more classic look. Here, a selection of transparent pale blue buttons and beads has been used to create a subtle design that would work particularly well with an evening outfit. The choker is given additional visual interest by combining square buttons with round beads so that the different shapes offset each other. Using the same buttons and beads in pretty pastel colours would create a great daytime choker.

CHAPTER TWO

Bracelets and Earrings

In this chapter you will find projects ranging from the simplicity of novelty buttons wired onto clip-on findings to make cute Teddy earrings (page 81) for a child, to a combination of delicate threads and transparent buttons in our sophisticated Dangle Earrings (page 98). Knit together tiny beads and fasten them with one dramatic button to create our glamorous Knitted Band (page 86) bracelet, or use several strands of beading wire to create clusters of buttons to wind around your wrist in Floral Garland (page 52).

Floral Garland

These delightful iridescent stem buttons look like the tightly furled petals of a flower. Interspersed with glass leaves, they create a delicate floral wreath for your wrist. The matching earrings are very easy to make and finish the ensemble beautifully. The blue and purple colour scheme can be swapped for more natural shades if you prefer. Simply select buttons in your favourite colour and type of flower, and team them with green leaves and brown-toned beads to give the effect of flowers growing on a stalk. Gold findings work best with this type of colour scheme. Make sure you use glass leaves with a hole running horizontally through the top so they sit flat and make the bracelet comfortable to wear.

materials
(BRACELET)

8 flower stem buttons
14 glass leaves
38 x 6/0 clear glass beads
32 x 8/0 turquoise glass beads
50cm (1$\frac{1}{2}$ft) fine beading wire
1 T-bar fastener
4 French crimps

materials
(EARRINGS)

2 stem flower buttons
2 glass leaves
2 tiny glass flower beads
2 x 6/0 clear glass beads
4 x 8/0 turquoise glass beads
2 x 3mm silver-plated balls
2 x 2mm silver-plated balls
20cm (8in) 0.6mm
   silver-plated wire
2 sterling silver earwires

tools

wire cutters
crimping pliers
round nose pliers
snipe nose pliers

techniques

crimping, page 126
closed loops, page 123

Bracelet

1 Cut the beading wire into two equal lengths. Holding both lengths together, work two ends of wire through one crimp and one clear bead, then another crimp and another clear bead. Pass the threads through one section of the fastener, then back through both crimps and beads. Squeeze the crimps with crimping pliers, then trim the ends of the thread.

2 Working with both strands together, thread on three clear beads, with a turquoise bead between them. Thread on the first button.

3 Divide the strands of beading wire and thread on one clear and then one turquoise bead followed by a leaf onto each strand.

4 Add a turquoise then a clear bead onto each strand, then bring the strands together again and thread them both through the next button. Continue in this way, separating the strands to add the leaves and beads, then bringing them together for each button.

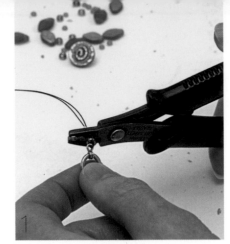

5 As you work, regularly push the beads and buttons down the beading wire towards the fastener to keep them as close together as possible. Make sure that all the buttons face upwards.

6 After the final button has been added, bring the strands together to thread on the last few beads and the remaining French crimps, matching the order at the other end of the bracelet. Pass both strands through the remaining section of the fastener, then back through the first two beads and crimps. Pull the strands so that everything is as tight as possible, then squeeze the crimps with crimping pliers and trim the ends of the wire.

Earrings

1 Cut the wire into two equal lengths and thread one piece through a glass leaf. Bend up about 3cm (1¼in) of wire on one side of the leaf.

2 Cross the wires and wind the short end around the longer end above the leaf. This is basically the same as making a closed loop.

1

6

2

3 After a few wraps, clip off the end of the wire. Use snipe nose pliers to press the sharp end back into the wraps. Pull up the remaining wire to straighten it.

4 Thread on the button, followed by half the beads and silver-plated balls in an arrangement you like. Finish the earring by making a closed loop at the top. Wrap the end of the wire around the stem of wire below the loop as many times as you can, then clip off the end of the wire. This tight wrapping means that there will be no movement between the beads and the button, so the earring will retain its shape.

5 Finish by adding an earwire, making sure you use pliers to twist open the loop on the earwire sideways so that the wire is not weakened. Follow Steps 1–5 to make a second earring, matching the arrangement of beads on the first earring. Use pliers to twist the earrings so that they hang well.

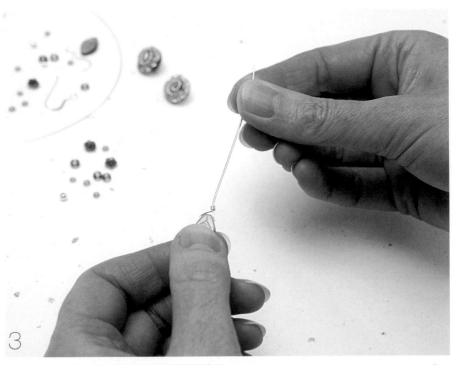

3

4

5

VARIATION The base of this necklace is made by threading glass leaves, coloured beads and tiny glass flowers together in a symmetrical design. At the centre of the necklace is a single button pendant. To add the button, thread it onto a short length of wire, wrapping one end of the wire around the other to secure the button. Form a closed loop at the other end of the wire and thread it onto the centre of the necklace. Make sure that the pendant section is long enough to hang below the leaves.

Charm Bracelet

Many people keep a special button box where they store leftover buttons. As you become more enthusiastic about making button jewellery, you will soon find that your collection of buttons grows very quickly. This bracelet is a great way to use leftover buttons from other projects, or the spare buttons that you get when you buy a new item of clothing. All of the buttons used here have a pearlescent sheen and are in neutral colours, but your selection of buttons can be as crazy or as restrained as you like. The only other embellishment you need is a handful of beads, and again you can use leftovers from other projects. Choose a silver- or gold-plated chain, depending on the colour scheme of the buttons and beads, together with wire to match the chain.

materials
25–30 small buttons
40 x 8/0 beads
20cm (8in) large-linked chain
2–2.5m (7–8ft) 0.6mm wire
  to match the chain
bolt ring or trigger fastener

tools
round nose pliers
snipe nose pliers
wire cutters

techniques
wiring to hang, page 125
closed loops, page 123

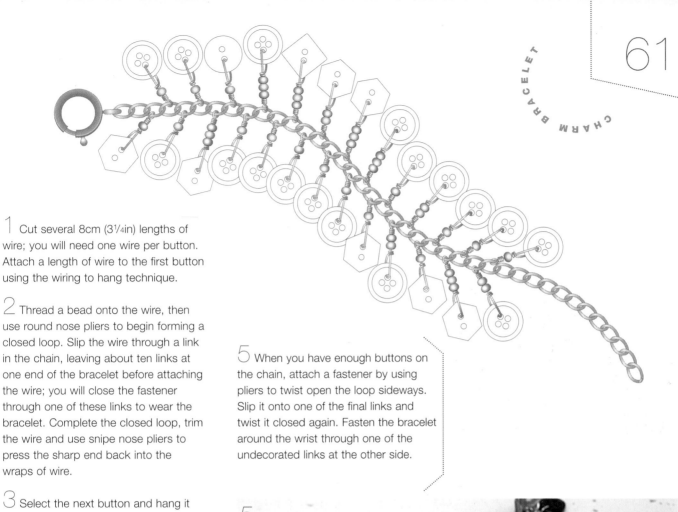

1 Cut several 8cm (3¹⁄₄in) lengths of wire; you will need one wire per button. Attach a length of wire to the first button using the wiring to hang technique.

2 Thread a bead onto the wire, then use round nose pliers to begin forming a closed loop. Slip the wire through a link in the chain, leaving about ten links at one end of the bracelet before attaching the wire; you will close the fastener through one of these links to wear the bracelet. Complete the closed loop, trim the wire and use snipe nose pliers to press the sharp end back into the wraps of wire.

3 Select the next button and hang it from another wire with a couple of beads above it. Attach this wire to the next link in the chain in the same way as you did in Step 2.

4 Continue adding wired buttons to the chain in this way, varying the length of the wires by adding between one and three beads above the buttons. Make sure that you add the wires to the same side of the links as you progress.

5 When you have enough buttons on the chain, attach a fastener by using pliers to twist open the loop sideways. Slip it onto one of the final links and twist it closed again. Fasten the bracelet around the wrist through one of the undecorated links at the other side.

5

Memory Bracelet

This striking bracelet can be made with any collection of stem buttons: look in charity shops for old and unusual buttons with stems. A selection of blue, green and red buttons with a swirling leaf design has been used here, with larger buttons positioned at the centre of the bracelet. The exact number of buttons and beads needed will depend on how many loops you want your bracelet to have. Memory wire is a very strong, prewound wire that remembers its shape, hence the name. Simply spread open the loops to slip the bracelet onto your wrist and then let it go; the wire will return to its original shape and stay in place on the wrist. You must always use special tools when working with memory wire, or strong old tools; never risk your usual wireworking tools because they are delicate and you risk damaging them.

materials
20 stem buttons
approx 70 x 6/0 glass beads
approx 20 x 4mm round beads
2–3 loops of bracelet-size
   memory wire

tools
very strong wire cutters
strong round or snipe nose pliers

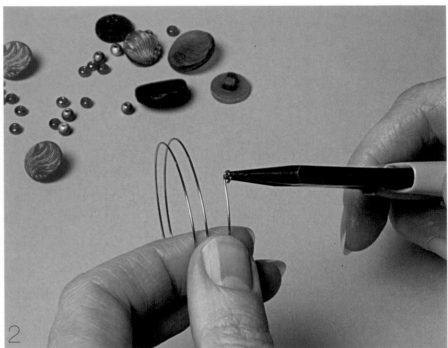

1 Cut the required length of memory wire with strong wire cutters. Be careful because memory wire is very sharp.

2 Hold one end of the wire with sturdy pliers, then twist the pliers around to roll one end of the wire outwards to form a small loop. Be careful of your hands.

3 Thread two 6/0 beads and then one button onto the wire. The bracelet shown here starts with smaller buttons and progresses to larger ones, but this is not essential.

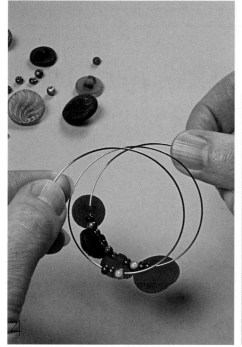

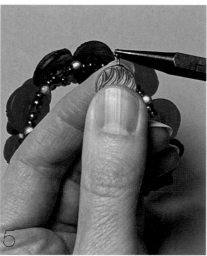

4 Continue to thread buttons onto the wire, adding enough beads between to ensure they sit comfortably together.

5 Give everything a little shake and push the buttons and beads together to make sure that there are no gaps before you roll the end. Leave just enough wire at the end of the memory wire so that you can roll it around to match the loop on the other end.

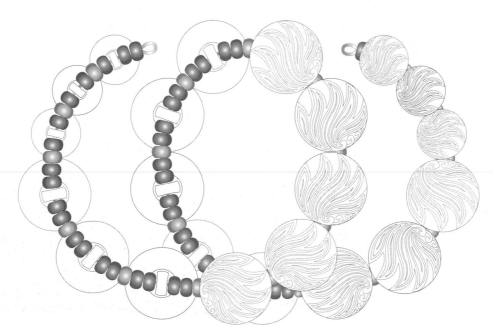

Wedding Days

In this design, a sumptuous collection of pearlescent white stem buttons has been woven together with silver seed beads and clear magatama beads to create a really lush effect. Magatama beads are teardrop shaped with off-centre holes, so they give the bracelet an organic feeling of movement. It is worth experimenting with which magatama beads you put together until you find ones that will sit well as a group. Here, hexagonal buttons are teamed with round buttons in two different sizes, again enhancing the organic texture of the piece. You could very easily expand the length of the design to make a matching choker. The bracelet is closed with a heart-shaped fastener, making it perfect for a bride or her bridesmaids.

materials

16 stem buttons in 3 sizes
approx 60 clear magatama beads
approx 70 x 8/0 silver beads
6 x 6/0 clear beads
90cm (3ft) extra-fine beading wire
4 French crimps
1 heart-shaped T-bar fastener

tools

crimping pliers
wire cutters or strong scissors

techniques

crimping, page 126

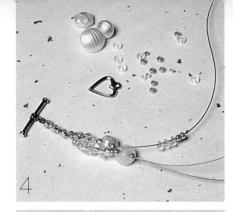

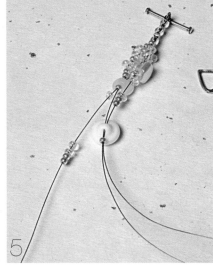

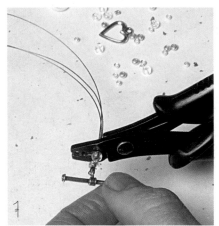

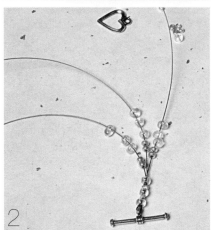

2 Thread on a third 6/0 bead. (If you want a longer bracelet, add more 6/0 beads at this point.) When you are ready, separate the strands and thread two 8/0 beads and then three magatama beads onto each strand.

3 On one of the strands, add another 8/0 bead, three magatamas and another two 8/0 beads. Join the other two strands of beading wire together and thread on one 8/0 bead, one button and another 8/0 bead. (Adjust the number of 8/0 beads so everything sits together well.)

4 Now join two different strands together and thread on a second button with another 8/0 bead after it. On the remaining single strand, add three magatama beads and two 8/0 beads.

5 Separate the beading wires again, then thread two different strands through one of the larger buttons and one 8/0 bead. Again, put three magatama and two 8/0 beads onto the remaining single strand.

1 Cut the beading wire into three equal pieces. Holding all three strands together, thread them through one crimp and one 6/0 bead, then another crimp and 6/0 bead. Thread the strands through one section of the fastener, then back through the beads and crimps. Squeeze the crimps with crimping pliers, then trim the ends of the wire.

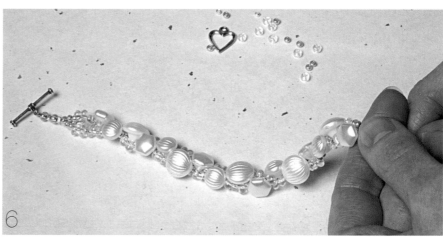

6 Continue in this way until you have added all of the buttons. Regularly push the beads and buttons down the beading wire to keep the design firm.

7 Separate the strands and add three magatama and two 8/0 beads to each strand. Bring the strands back together and thread all three through a 6/0 bead.

8 Push the work together one more time, using pliers to help you draw the beading wire tight. Attach this end of the bracelet to the heart section of the fastener using crimps and 6/0 beads as you did in Step 1. Clip off the ends of the beading wire.

materials

- 2 large two-hole star buttons
- 2 medium two-hole star buttons
- 4 small two-hole star buttons
- 10 x 8/0 beads
- 82cm (33in) 0.6mm
  silver-plated wire
- 2 sterling silver earwires

tools

- wire cutters
- round nose pliers
- snipe nose pliers

techniques

closed loops, page 123
wiring to hang, page 125

Simple Stars

Stunning star-shaped buttons in three different sizes are used here to make these fun earrings. Making them is a good way to practise your wiring techniques. If wirework feels a little awkward at first, practise wrapping and forming loops on a few spare pieces of wire, running the pliers over the wire several times to smooth it out. Make sure that you do not wrap the wire too close to the buttons, as this will prevent each section of the earring moving freely about. The shiny shell buttons will catch and reflect the light as the earrings move, drawing attention to how pretty they are. You can, of course, select different shaped buttons, and combine them with beads in either toning or contrasting colours, depending on the effect you want to achieve.

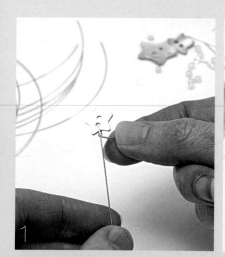

1 Cut one 10cm (4in), three 8cm (3¼in) and one 7cm (2¾in) lengths of wire for each earring. Using a 8cm (3¼in) length of wire, hang one of the small star buttons from it using the wiring to hang technique.

2 Thread on a bead, then leave a gap of about 1.5cm (½in) before using pliers to form a closed loop.

3 Repeat this process with another 8cm (3¼in) piece of wire and small star button, making the dangle a slightly different length from the first one. Hang a medium button onto a 7cm (2¾in) length of wire in the same way, but do not leave a gap in the wire this time.

4 When you have made all the hanging stars for one earring, attach them to the big star button. Make a bigger loop near one end of a 10cm (4in) length of wire. Thread the hanging stars onto this loop, then wrap the short end of the wire around the long end to secure them. Trim the wire and use snipe nose pliers to press the sharp end into the wraps.

5 Thread a bead onto the wire, then pass the wire through the bottom hole of the big star button so that the loop faces forwards. Make sure that you leave enough space to wrap the wire below the big button without losing movement. Bend the wire down the back of the button, then wrap it around the wire in the usual way. Trim and neaten the wire as before.

6 Take a 8cm (3¼in) length of wire and thread it through the top hole of the button. Fold the wire and wrap it above the button using the wiring to hang technique. Do not wrap the wire too close to the button or the earring will lose some of its movement. Thread on another bead and form a closed loop above it.

7 Finish by attaching the earwire. Do this by using pliers to twist open the loop on the earwire sideways. Slip the earring onto the loop, then twist it closed again. Make a second earring in the same way. You may need to twist the wire a small amount to adjust the way that the earrings hang.

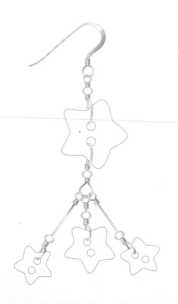

VARIATION While the star shell earrings use neutral colours for a subtle look, this blue button and crystal bead adaptation creates a much more dramatic effect. Both versions use monochromatic colour schemes, but the choice of a vivid primary colour radically alters the finished result. Interest is added to the design by the combination of angular multifaceted crystals with smooth round buttons. The buttons have a gentle curve across their surface that highlights their lustrous finish.

Big Buttons

This simple but dramatic bracelet could be made with any large striking buttons: Here, shocking pink buttons have been teamed with turquoise thread to increase the boldness of the bracelet, but you could tone down the colours and use smaller buttons to make a more subtle piece of jewellery. The Black Beauty choker on page 34 uses the same threading technique, so why not make a choker to match the bracelet? The techniques used to make this bracelet are so simple that you may be tempted to make several in different colour schemes. Enjoy experimenting with buttons in different materials. Shiny shell buttons would look very different from these bright plastic buttons, or you could use a selection of novelty shaped buttons instead.

materials

8 large two-hole buttons
4 x 6/0 beads
25cm (10in) thick polyester thread
1 T-bar fastener
4 French crimps

tools

crimping pliers
scissors

techniques

crimping, page 126

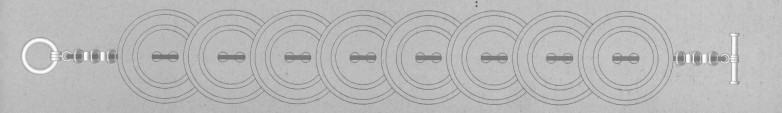

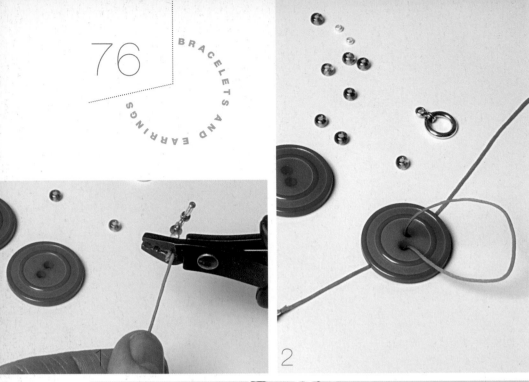

3 Continue adding buttons in this way, spacing them evenly so that they overlap and sit together neatly.

4 When you reach the other end of the bracelet, thread on alternating crimps and beads as before. Take the thread through the other section of the fastener, back through the crimps and beads, and squeeze them with the pliers to complete the bracelet. Trim the ends of thread if necessary.

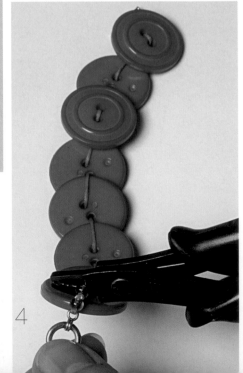

1 Pass one end of the thread through one crimp and bead, then another crimp and bead. Pass the thread through one section of the fastener, then back through the crimps and beads. Squeeze the crimp with the crimping pliers.

2 Thread on the first button by passing the thread up through the first hole to the front of the button, then down through the second hole to the back of the button.

VARIATION You can make a bracelet using the same technique but with four-hole buttons for a slightly different look. Run one thread through the top pairs of holes and another thread through the bottom pairs. Attach both threads to the fastener in the way described in the main project, but check that the beads and crimps are large enough to accommodate four ends of thread. The buttons used here have irregular black striations, so black thread was the obvious choice to go with them.

Teddies and Toys

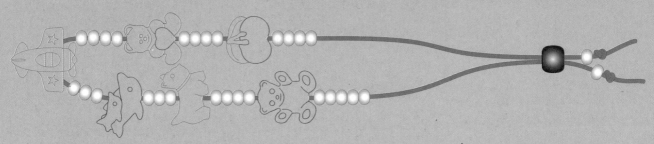

This quick and easy bracelet is a great project to make with a small child. You can cut the thong and tie the knots if necessary, then allow the child to arrange the buttons and beads in their own design. Plastic novelty buttons are cheap but durable and are widely available. Teddy bears, dogs, planes, dolphins and cherries are just a few of the many designs on sale. You will probably find that choosing the selection of buttons with your child is as much fun as making the bracelet together. The number of silver beads you require may vary, depending on the size of the novelty buttons. Dangle a pair of your child's favourite buttons from earring clips to make a matching jewellery set, but take care when using wire and pliers near young children.

materials
(BRACELET)
6 novelty stem buttons
approx 30 x 4mm silver beads
1 strong bead with a 2mm hole
30–40cm (12–16in) 1mm leather
   or cotton thong

materials
(EARRINGS)
2 novelty stem buttons
10 x 4mm silver beads
2 headpins
2 clip earring findings

tools
wire cutters
round nose pliers

Bracelet

1 Cut the thong to the required length, allowing a little extra in case the end you use for threading becomes frayed and you have to trim it. Thread on five silver beads and the first button.

2 Continue adding beads and buttons until you are happy with the arrangement. You will probably need to use different amounts of beads between the buttons, depending on their design. Make sure that you save seven beads to use at the end.

3 When you have added the final button, thread on five beads to make a symmetrical design. Thread both ends of the thong through the strong bead.

4 Thread a silver bead on each end of the thong. Check that the bracelet is just large enough to slip on, then tie a knot to hold the silver beads in place, trimming the thong if necessary. To wear the bracelet, tighten it by sliding the strong bead towards the wrist.

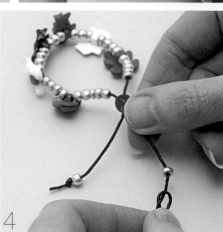

Earrings

1 Thread one silver bead, one button and then four more silver beads onto a headpin. Cut the pin to leave about 8mm (¹/₄in) of wire above the beads.

2 Use round nose pliers to form a loop above the beads. First bend the wire at a 45-degree angle towards you.

3 Then use the pliers to roll the wire away from you. You may need to perform this movement twice before you get a complete loop. Try to get the loop as tight to the beads as possible so that they will not move about.

4 Use pliers to twist open the loop on the earclip sideways. Slip the earring onto the loop, then twist the loop closed again. Make a second earring in the same way.

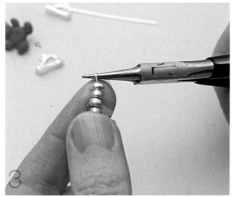
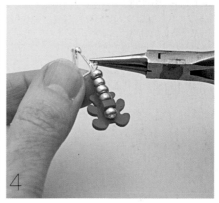

Abalone Birds

Little birds made from abalone shell are used to create this very special bracelet. The matching abalone shell buttons have lovely markings on them, with iridescent peacock colours that glint and gleam as the light catches them at different angles. Square and circular buttons are alternated to provide changing frames for the bird centrepieces. If you have trouble finding birds like those

featured here, any interesting beads will look good running across such stunningly beautiful buttons as these. The small blue and silver beads can be threaded randomly between the birds and buttons, or you could create a regular colour pattern if you prefer. Choose bead colours that will enhance the delicate birds and buttons rather than detract attention from them.

materials
- **3 round two-hole buttons**
- **3 square two-hole buttons**
- **6 through-drilled birds**
- **approx 40 x 8/0 blue beads**
- **approx 20 tiny silver beads**
- **50cm (1¹/₂ft) fine beading wire**
- **7cm (2³/₄in) 0.6mm silver-plated wire**
- **small length of large-linked chain**
- **2 French crimps**
- **trigger or lobster clasp fastener**

tools
wire cutters
crimping pliers
round nose pliers
snipe nose pliers

techniques
crimping, page 126
closed loops, page 123

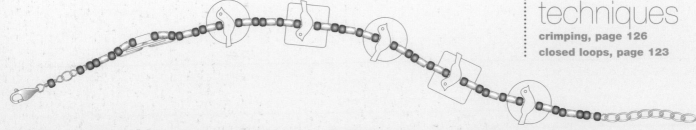

1 Cut the beading wire into two equal lengths, then cut the chain so that you have one single link and a short length of about six or seven links. Holding both lengths of wire together, thread one crimp and one blue bead onto the end. Thread the wire through the last link in the longer length of chain, then back through the bead and crimp. Squeeze the crimp with crimping pliers.

2 Thread six or seven blue and silver beads onto both strands of wire, then separate the wires to add the first two-hole button. Thread one strand of wire up through the first button hole from below, then down through the second button hole.

3 Thread more beads and a bird onto the second strand of wire, using sufficient beads to match the width of the button and to place the bird right in the centre.

4 Bring the two strands back together and thread them through a few more of the blue and silver beads.

5 Separate the strands again to add the next button in the same way as before, threading beads and a bird onto the front strand. Continue in this way for all of the buttons and birds.

6 When the last button has been added, thread on a few more small beads to create a symmetrical design with the first end of the bracelet. Attach this end of the bracelet to the single chain link using a bead and crimp as before. Cut off the extra lengths of beading wire.

7 Thread the silver-plated wire through the single chain link and use pliers to form a closed loop around the link. Thread on a small bead.

8 Finish by forming another closed loop above the bead, slipping the clasp onto the loop before wrapping the wire around the stem. You can fasten the clasp through any of the chain links on the other side of the bracelet.

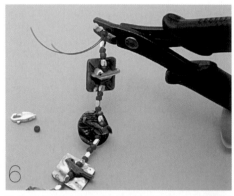

VARIATION This matching pendant layers three abalone shell buttons together, with an unusual triangular button between a pair of round buttons. The three buttons are wired together, with a silver bead and hanging loop above, then the finished pendant is slipped onto a long silver snake chain. If you prefer, use a bird button in place of the round button at the centre of the pendant to match the abalone bracelet more exactly.

Knitted Band

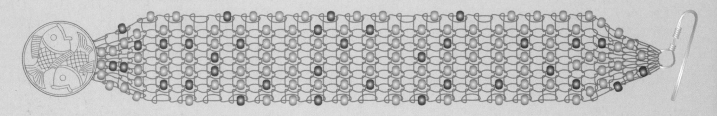

This is an intriguing way to make a bracelet. With a few basic knitting skills—casting on and knit stitch—you can create a band of beaded wire that will fit around the wrist. Knitting with wire seems very untidy when you first start, but as the band gets longer, you will be able to pull it into a more attractive, uniform shape. Try to keep the stitches loose on the needles or you will find it difficult to

knit. Thick blunt-ended sewing needles are used here as knitting needles, but if you cannot find anything suitable, you could try cocktail sticks instead. The small beads have been knitted into every other row so that the finished result is a decorative combination of beads and wire. A large ornate button is the perfect fastener for the bracelet.

materials
1 ornate stem button
150–200 x 8/0 beads
1 reel of 0.3mm beading wire
25cm (10in) 0.6mm
  silver-plated wire

tools
2 sturdy needles, at least 7cm
  (2³⁄₄in) long
wire cutters
round nose pliers
snipe nose pliers

techniques
closed loops, page 123

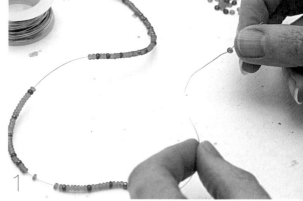

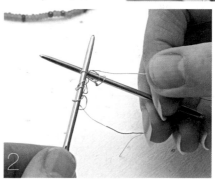

1 Keeping the wire on the reel, thread the beads onto the wire until you have covered about 30cm (12in) of wire with them. Save one of the beads for the fastener.

2 Push the beads up towards the reel to keep them out of the way. Leaving a 15cm (6in) tail of wire, cast on six stitches, making them as loose as possible on the needles. Knit one row without any beads, keeping the stitches as loose as you can.

3 Slide six beads closer to the knitting, then knit a second row. Slide the beads one at a time up the wire so that one bead sits between each pair of stitches. The knitting will look very rough and tangled at this stage, but you will be able to pull it into better shape as the knitting gets longer.

4 Knit a third row without any beads. Alternating beaded and unbeaded rows will make knitting with wire easier, but you could add beads on each row if you prefer. If you do, put double the amount of beads onto the wire at the start.

5 Continue alternating beaded and unbeaded rows until the knitted band is long enough to fit around your wrist, pulling the knitting into shape as you go.

6 Cut a 10cm (4in) length of 0.6mm wire and bend it about halfway along to form a large open loop. Slip the stitches from the needle onto the loop of wire. Wind the end of the fine knitting wire around one side of the loop. Clip it off and then press in the end with a pair of snipe nose pliers.

7 Work both ends of the 0.6mm wire through the button hole, then wrap the wire around until you are happy that the button is secure. Clip off the wire as close to the button as possible so that it will not be scratchy, pressing the end into the wraps with snipe nose pliers.

8 Use the remaining 15cm (6in) length of 0.6mm wire to pick up the stitches at the other end of the knitted band, then bend the end of the wire around to form a large closed loop.

9 Thread a bead onto the wire above the loop, then fold the wire in half about 4cm (1¹⁄₂in) from the bead. Straighten the two ends of wire together, then wrap the end of the folded piece around the wire above the bead.

10 Use pliers to bend the doubled wire into a hook shape that will fasten around the button at the other end of the band to hold the bracelet in place.

VARIATION Experiment with your beaded knitting and have fun working on the effect you want to create. The main project has beads knitted into alternate rows, but this variation shows what the bracelet looks like with beads knitted into every row. A few unbeaded rows are left at each end of the band so the beads do not interfere with the button fastening. The large vintage black button is complemented by gold and black beads on a network of silver wire.

materials

1 decorative stem button
approx 100 x 4mm cube beads
approx 100 each 6/0 beads in two
   colours
8m (27ft) strong polyester thread
20cm (8in) piping
nail polish or glue (optional)

tools

scissors
fine needle
sticky tape

Mona Lisa Smile

This fantastic Mona Lisa button was handmade in California and deserves a special treatment. Here, it has been used as the fastener for a woven bangle of beads. The beads are woven into a tube using peyote stitch. Also known as gourd stitch, this is a relatively simple beadweaving technique. You can use any beads with central holes large enough to accommodate a doubled length of thread, but you will find it easier to follow the workings of the stitch if you use three different colours. Select bead colours that pick up the colours in the button you are using. You can buy the piping from a craft store, or be inventive: the piping used here is actually a handle from a smart carrier bag.

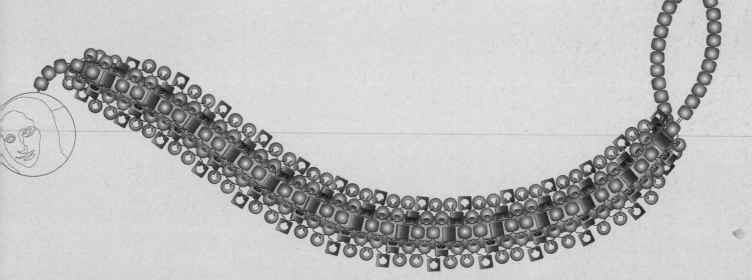

1 Cut the required length of piping; you need 4cm (1½in) less than the bracelet length. It is a good idea to put some glue or nail polish onto the ends of the piping to stop it from fraying. Cut the first length of thread; an arm's length should feel comfortable to work with. Thread it onto the needle and work with it doubled. Put a small piece of tape across the threads about 20cm (8in) from the end. Slide the first three beads onto the thread, one in each colour.

2 Use the tip of the needle to pick up another bead in the first colour, then take the needle back through the first bead, from the tape end downwards. Pick up a bead in the second colour, then thread the needle down through the second bead. Pick up a bead in the third colour, then thread the needle down through the third bead. Pick up a bead in the first colour again, then thread the needle down through the fourth bead and so on. Continue to work in this manner.

3 For the first few rows, the beadwork will seem rather messy, but you will soon see a small tube begin to form.

4 Push one end of the piping into the tube and secure it with a few stitches.

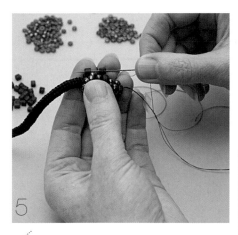

5

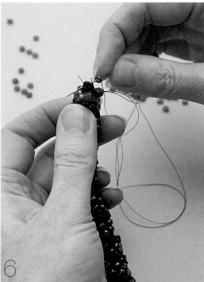

6

7

8

8 Remove the tape from the threads at the other end of the bracelet, then add enough round beads to create a loop that will be just large enough to go over the button. Finish off this thread in the same way as you did on the other side. Trim off any loose threads.

5 Continue adding rows of peyote stitch as before, working around the piping. Occasionally take the needle through the piping to secure the beads to it. When you run out of thread and need to add new length, secure the old and new threads with a few stitches into the piping.

6 When the piping is completely covered, weave another row of peyote stitch to cover the end of the piping. Work through these last beads several times to make them firmer.

7 Thread on three more round beads of any colour, then thread on the button. Take the needle through the button hole once again, then thread back down through the last three round beads, down through some of the weaving and into the piping to secure the thread. Trim the end of thread.

Vintage Style

Italian vintage buttons are threaded onto two coils of memory wire to create a simple but stylish bracelet, with a larger central button. You will need to hunt in charity shops or antique markets to find this sort of button, but it is worth the effort because you will achieve a very special result.

Memory wire is a strong, precoiled wire that retains its shape. Be careful when working with memory wire because it is extremely sharp; it will also wreck ordinary tools, so use heavy-duty ones or strong old tools. The arrangement of beads and buttons for the bracelet was decided upon in advance, so that

the bracelet could be threaded working from one end to the other. You may find it easier to plan your own vintage bracelet in the same way, rather than working out from a central button and creating the design as you go.

materials

**5 buttons with a stem or
  cloth back**
20 small cube beads
96 x 8/0 beads
**2–3 loops of bracelet-size
  memory wire**

tools

very strong wire cutters
strong round or snipe nose pliers
strong needle

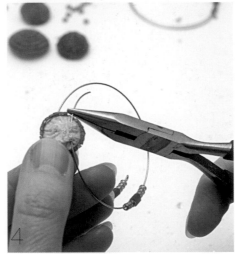

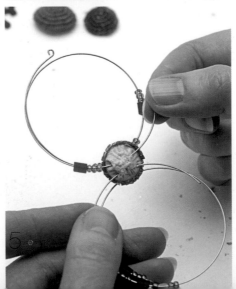

1 Cut the required length of memory wire with strong wire cutters. Be careful because memory wire is very sharp.

2 Pick up the first section of wire and hold one end of the wire with sturdy pliers. Twist the pliers around to roll one end of the wire outwards to form a small loop. Thread on the first selection of beads. Repeat this process with the second coil of memory wire.

3 Use a needle to make holes through the back of the buttons if necessary so that you can thread the buttons onto the wire. You may find it easier to make each hole immediately before threading.

4 Work the first section of wire through one side of the first button. You may find that it helps to use pliers to push or pull the wire through.

5 Push the other section of wire through the back of the same button.

6 Add more beads in the required design, then add another button. Continue in this way until you reach the other end of the bracelet.

7 When all the buttons and beads have been added, clip the wires so that you have about 8mm (¹/₄in) of wire left. Use pliers to roll these ends outwards to form a small loop as before.

Dangle Earrings

You could use this design with many different types of buttons and beads. Here, sweet little heart-shaped beads are combined with multifaceted transparent buttons in matching pastel shades to create a light, springtime look. However, you could use all sorts of combinations, from swirling abalone shell buttons to funky bright plastic ones. The earrings would look equally good if made using a mixture of leftover buttons from other projects. Just remember that they should not be so heavy that they are uncomfortable to wear. Black polyester thread works well with our transparent buttons but you could use white thread for an even lighter effect.

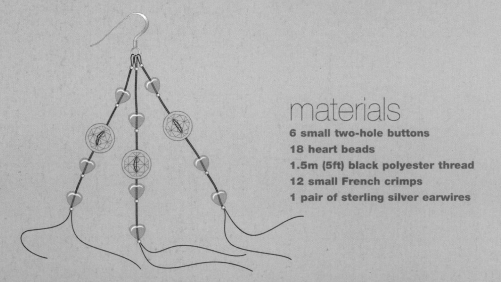

materials
6 small two-hole buttons
18 heart beads
1.5m (5ft) black polyester thread
12 small French crimps
1 pair of sterling silver earwires

tools
crimping pliers
snipe or round nose pliers
12cm (5in) fine beading wire

techniques
crimping, page 126

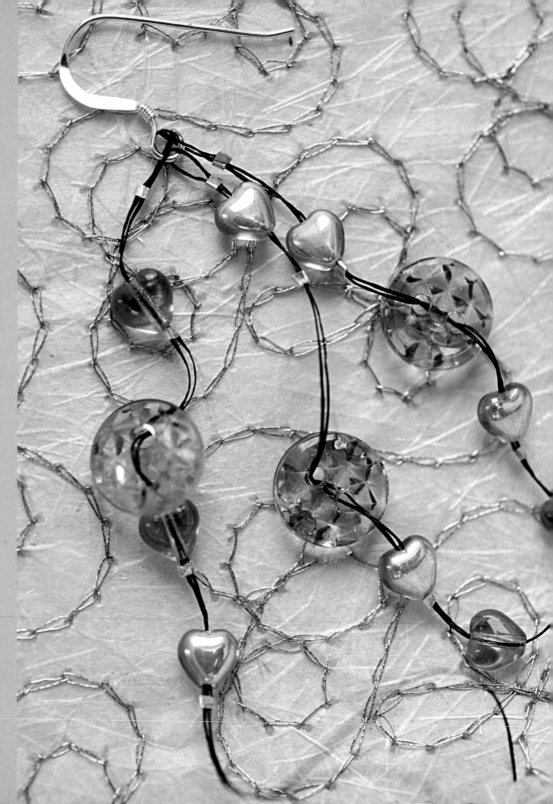

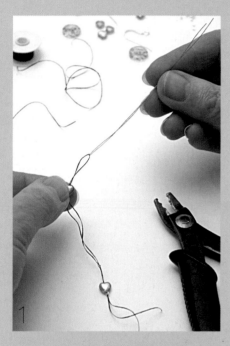

1 Cut the thread into six equal lengths. Fold the first length in half and loop the beading wire through it. Slide a French crimp down the beading wire and onto the thread. Use pliers to squeeze the crimp onto the thread about 8cm (3in) from the fold. Make sure this is very secure because it will hold everything in place. Using the wire to help you thread on the various elements, thread on the first heart bead, then leave a small gap and add another crimp and heart.

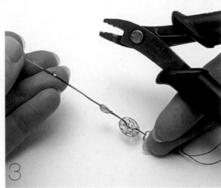

2 Thread on one of the buttons and secure another crimp above it. Remove the beading wire while squeezing the crimp if necessary.

3 Thread on another heart, then squeeze a crimp about 3–4mm (1/8in) from the top of the strand.

4 Make another strand to match the first one; one strand will be used in each earring. Make two more pairs of strands to complete the dangles for each earring. The three pairs of strands should be slightly different lengths.

5 Separate the strands so that you have three different strands for each earring. Use pliers to twist open the loop on the earwire sideways. Hang the

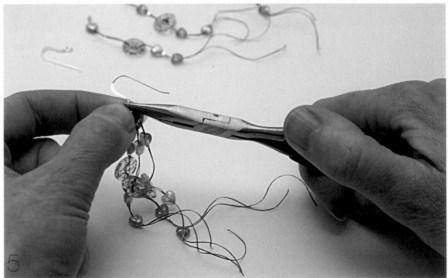

three strands from this loop, then twist the loop closed again. Complete the second earring in the same way. Trim the bottom of the threads if you want to.

DANGLE EARRINGS

VARIATION Pretty pastel hearts have been combined here with transparent plastic buttons embedded with silver glitter to create a glitzy pair of earrings. Although the overall colour scheme is not drastically different from the main project, the change of buttons definitely makes these earrings more suitable for a party. Try teaming the buttons with different types of beads, such as stars and crescent moons. You could also make a third set of strands to suspend from a necklace as a pendant.

Ocean Earrings

These shell-shaped buttons are too tempting not to use for jewellery-making. They would work well in all sorts of pieces, from necklaces to bracelets, but they make particularly distinctive earrings. Keeping to a sea theme, the buttons are combined with pearl beads in toning shades of pewter, with complementary silver wire holding the various elements together. Shells and pearls are especially good for making jewellery because of their beautiful sheen, and nowadays they are both available in many different colours and sizes. However, any attractive buttons and beads can be used in this design. If the button is shaped, like these shells, always make sure that you thread the wires through it correctly so that the button is the right way up.

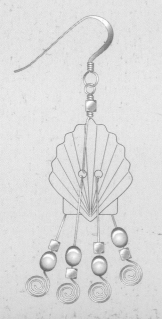

materials
2 two-hole shell-shaped buttons
8 small pearls
10 silver cube beads
60cm (2ft) 0.4mm silver-plated wire
2 sterling silver earwires

tools
wire cutters
round nose pliers
snipe nose pliers

techniques
single coils, page 122
closed loops, page 123

1 Cut the wire into six equal lengths. Form a single coil at the bottom of one wire. Slide a pearl and silver bead onto the wire, then thread the wire through one hole in the button from the front. Make sure that the button is the right way up, then smooth the wire against the button on both sides.

2 Form a single coil at the end of a second piece of wire, then thread on a silver bead and pearl. Thread this wire through the same button hole as before, but this time thread from the back of the button. Smooth both wires up to the top of the button. Wrap one of the wires around the other a few times, allowing some space for movement, then trim the end of the wrapping wire.

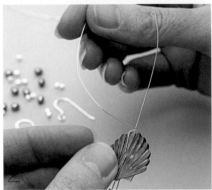

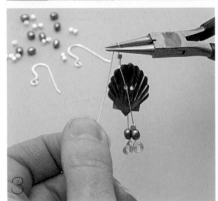

3 Thread a silver bead onto the remaining piece of wire above the button, then use pliers to form a closed loop above the bead. Trim the wire, then use snipe nose pliers to press the end of wire into the wraps below the closed loop.

4 Make a single coil in a third piece of wire, add a pearl and silver bead, then thread the wire through the other hole in the button from front to back. Bend this wire down at the back, add a pearl and silver bead again, then form another single coil at this end of the wire.

5 Use pliers to twist open the loop on an earwire sideways. Slip the closed loop of the earring onto the earwire, then squeeze the earwire loop closed. Follow Steps 1–5 to make a second earring in the same way.

VARIATION This stylish necklace uses the same combination of nautilus shell buttons, silver cubes and pearl beads in shades of pewter as the Ocean Earrings. It is made using the same construction method as Pretty Pearls (page 10).

CHAPTER THREE

Pins and Hairslides

Making wearable pieces like the pins and hair decorations in this section is another exciting way to use buttons. Begin by purchasing readymade findings for brooches or hairslides from a bead or jewellery supplier, then consider how you can combine them with your favourite buttons. Wire big chunky buttons with brightly coloured beads to recreate the Mellow Yellow Hairslide (page 116) or make a simple piece like the Leather-backed Pin (page 112), featuring one knock-out button.

Flower Pin

A little cluster of flower buttons is wired together to form a small bouquet. This project is a little more difficult to make than some of the other designs, but it is very rewarding. Take your time when wiring the flowers to the pin clip to make sure that you do not prick yourself. Alternatively, you could attach the flowers to a hairslide finding. Pastel buttons and green wrapping wire make the perfect combination for a floral display, but any other selection of small buttons could be attached to a pin clip in the same way. Wear the bouquet for summer picnics, or make a few for special wedding guests to wear and save as keepsakes. You can use more or fewer flower stems if you wish, as long as they cover the pin clip. The design works best if you stick to an odd number of stems.

materials

7 two-hole flower buttons
90cm (3ft) 0.6mm silver-plated wire
40cm (16in) 0.7mm coloured wire
1 pin clip

tools

wire cutters
snipe nose pliers

techniques

coiling back, page 122

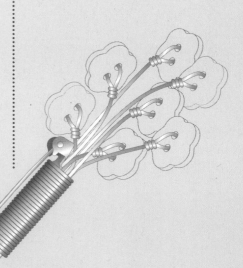

1 Cut the silver-plated wire into seven equal lengths. Fold over the top of the first piece and pull it through one of the buttons. You need about 3cm (1¼in) on the short end.

2 Cross the wires below the button, then wrap the short end firmly around the longer one a few times.

3 When the button feels secure, clip off the short end of wire. Use snipe nose pliers to press the sharp end into the wrapped wire. Repeat this process to add a wire stem to the remaining six flower buttons.

4 Run your fingers down the stems of the flowers to strengthen and straighten the wires.

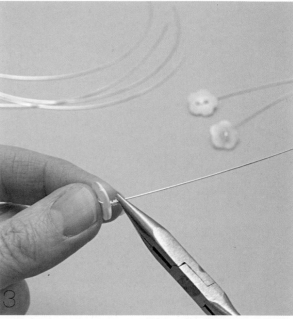

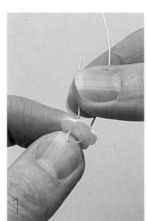

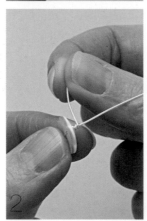

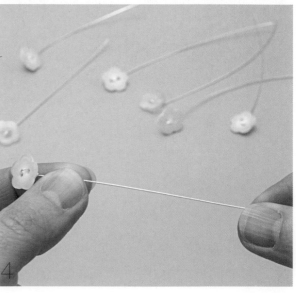

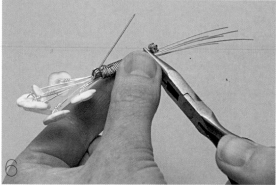

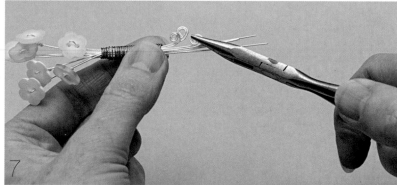

5 Group the wires in front of the pin clip, positioning them carefully so that the flower buttons are at different distances from the clip in a pleasing design. Try to get the wire stems flat against the pin clip. Open up the pin clip, and taking care that you do not prick yourself, wind the coloured wire tightly around the stems and clip. Start winding a little way down the wire and a little way along the pin clip so that you do not prevent the pin closing. You may find this a little awkward to do.

6 Continue winding the wire as firmly as you can, binding the stems onto the pin clip until you have covered the clip. Trim the ends of the coloured wire and use pliers to press the ends into the back of the work. Fasten the pin clip.

7 Trim the bottom of the flower stem wires to make them slightly different lengths, then coil each one back up towards the pin clip. Finish by adjusting the positions of the flower buttons and coils to make a pleasing arrangement.

Leather-backed Pin

This is a very quick way of using an interesting button to create a unique piece of jewellery. You can choose any size or design of button, and any type of fabric that will not fray. Leather is stylish, and you may be able to obtain a small sample from a fabric store. The creased surface of the leather enhances the design of the button, echoing the lines of pattern on its surface. You will need three circular items in gradually increasing diameters to use as templates for cutting out the three layers of leather. Do not worry if the circles of leather you cut out are not perfectly round. Leaving the edges a little uneven works perfectly with this design, though you may want to tidy the edges if you are using a different material where greater symmetry would look better.

materials

1 stem button
small piece of leather
80cm (31$\frac{1}{2}$in) strong polyester
    thread
1 pin clip

tools

round objects, such as buttons, to
    use as templates
pen
scissors
needle

1 Place the first round object onto the leather and draw around it. Cut out the circle, making it smooth or a little uneven around the edges, depending on what you prefer. Cut several circles, using slightly different diameter objects for each one to produce a layered effect. Three leather circles are used in the example shown here.

2 Fold each leather circle and make a tiny cut in the middle, just large enough for the stem of the button to fit through.

3 Layer the pieces of leather together. Place the button on top and push the stem through the layers. Using a doubled length of thread, sew a couple of times around the stem to secure the elements together.

4 Sew the stem of the button to the centre of the clip with a few stitches.

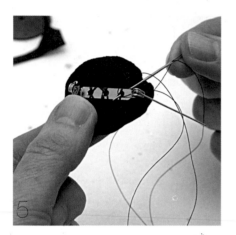

5 Sew along the rest of the clip, taking the needle through a little of the leather with each stitch as well as the holes in the brooch clip. Finish off the thread with a knot, then work the thread back through a few stitches and trim.

VARIATION This vintage button brooch is made from four circles of felt that have been cut out much more precisely and smoothly than the leather version, left. The felt circles do not have to be cut in the centre because a two-hole rather than a stem button has been used; simply sew through the button holes and layers of felt several times, before sewing the clip to the back. Finish the brooch with radiating lines of stitches around the outside of the felt using a doubled length of thread.

Mellow Yellow Hairslide

It is very simple to decorate a hairslide clip with buttons and beads. These have been sewn onto the slide, but for a slightly stiffer effect you could try wiring the buttons to the finding. However, as long as you use strong thread, sewing is very effective and there is no need to worry about the hairslide coming to pieces. Bright yellow buttons have been used here, making a cheerful hairslide that will brighten anyone's mood. The yellow beads are topped with miracle beads in alternating red and green. Also known as wonder beads, these lacquer-coated beads have a highly reflective mirror coating at their core, making them wonderfully shiny. However, you could use any type of bead you wish, together with any style and colour of button.

materials

6 two-hole buttons
**6 x 4mm miracle beads in two
  colours**
**80cm (32in) strong polyester
  thread**
1 hairslide clip

tools

needle
scissors

1 Thread the needle and knot the ends of the thread together. Take the needle through the hole at one end of the hairslide finding and through the doubled end of thread several times to secure the thread to the finding. Open the hairslide clip.

2 Take a button and, as you push the needle through the front of the finding, thread up through one button hole and then add a bead.

3 Take the needle down through the other button hole and underneath the front section of the finding.

4 Bring the thread back up on the other side of the finding and take it up through the next button. Add another bead, then take the needle down through the other button hole and around the front section of the finding as before. This is a rather fiddly process, but you will find it gets easier as you progress.

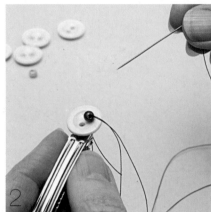

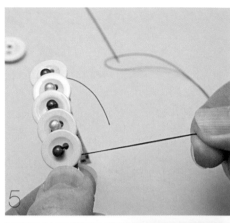

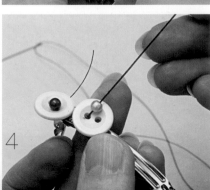

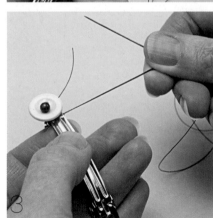

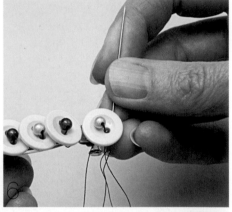

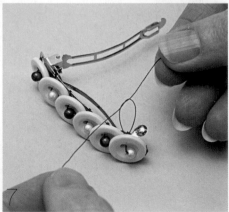

5 Continue to work along the hairslide, winding the thread tightly around it as you add the buttons and beads.

6 After adding the final button and bead, take the needle down through the hole at the other end of the hairslide.

7 Sew back between the buttons as many times as you can in order to make everything as firm as possible. Finish off by splitting the thread so that you can knot the ends together, then trim any loose ends.

VARIATIONS Instead of sewing the buttons and beads to the hairslide, you can wire them in place. Using plenty of silver-plated or coloured wire, thread on the buttons, beads and crystals, forming a single coil at each end of the wire (see page 122). Wrap the embellished wires around the hairslide clip, positioning the coils, buttons and beads attractively. Any little girl would love these slides: red and blue for a special day out, and sparkling silver for a princess-themed birthday party.

CHAPTER FOUR

Basic techniques

A range of basic wiring techniques is used in this book to create the jewellery designs. You will find a key to these on the project pages below the lists of tools and materials needed. The amounts given in this section are for practice pieces and may need to be adjusted when you come to make your final designs. Also included on these pages are the three knotting techniques used in the book.

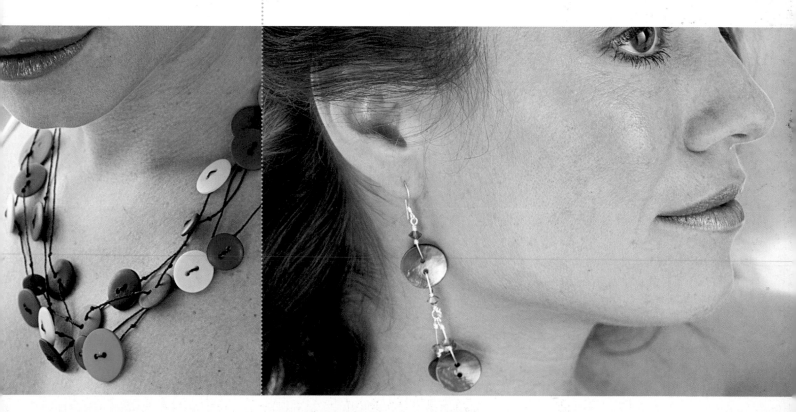

Coils

Single coils can be used decoratively on earrings and necklaces. It is a good idea to practise these coils with some extra wire before starting on your project.

Materials and tools
**15cm (6in) 0.6mm
   silver-plated wire
round nose pliers
snipe nose pliers**

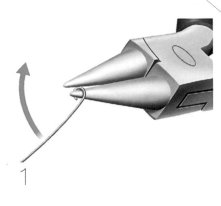

1 Make a tiny loop in the wire with the tip of the round nose pliers.

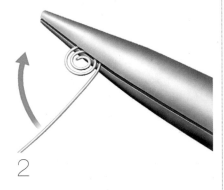

2 Hold the loop sideways with the snipe nose pliers. Hold the wire firmly, but not so tightly that you mark it. Use your finger and thumb to wind the wire around the first loop so that a coil begins to develop. Open the pliers to reposition the coil as you work.

3 When your coil is the desired size, use the snipe nose pliers to bend the wire away from the coil to an angle of 90 degrees.

Coiling back

The process of coiling back is very similar to making a single coil. These coils are generally used to complete a set of decorative coils.

Materials and tools
**15cm (6in) 0.6mm
   silver-plated wire
round nose pliers
snipe nose pliers**

---

1 Make a single coil following the instructions, left. Make a small loop in the straight end of the wire and hold it sideways in the snipe nose pliers. Use the strength from your wrist to coil the wire back up towards the first coil.

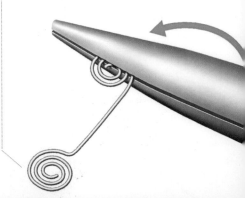

Double coils

These are similar to single coils, but are made in the centre of a wire. They can be linked onto wires and chains, or be threaded with beads and buttons on both sides.

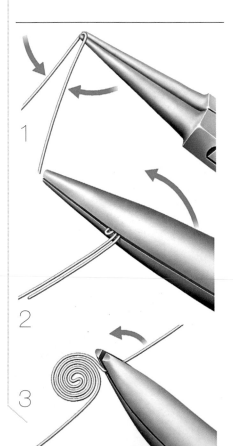

Materials and tools

25cm (10in) 0.6mm silver-plated wire
round nose pliers
snipe nose pliers

1 Use the tip of the round nose pliers to double over the wire in the centre of the length.

2 Use the snipe nose pliers to create a tiny loop. Holding the wire firmly in one hand, use the strength in your wrist to wind the wire around this small loop to build a coil.

3 When your coil is the desired size, bend one wire out at an angle of 90 degrees.

4 Wind the remaining wire to the other side of the coil, then bend that straight out as well.

Closed loops

Closed loops are the securest way to hang a bead or button, or to link a chain. Making them is the most important and versatile technique in all wire work and deserves to be practised.

Materials and tools

12cm (4³/₄in) 0.6mm silver-plated wire
round nose pliers
snipe nose pliers
wire cutters
beads

1 Use the tip of the round nose pliers to form a 'bow' shape in the wire about 3cm (1¹/₄in) from one end like the shape of an awareness ribbon.

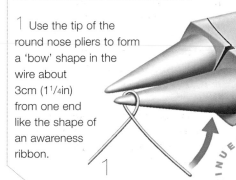

CONTINUED OVERLEAF

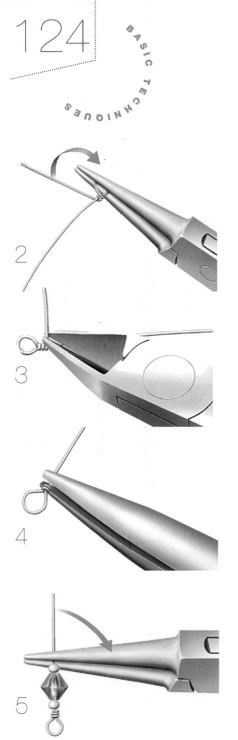

2

3

4

5

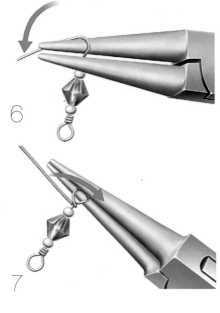

6

7

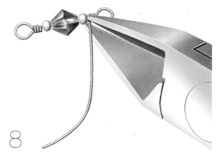

8

2 Hold the loop of the bow sideways in the pliers so that the longer end of the wire points straight out from the loop. Bend the shorter length of wire so that it is at right angles to the longer length. Holding the loop firmly in the pliers, use your finger and thumb to wrap the shorter length of wire under and over the longer one as shown. Repeat this two or three times, keeping the wraps neat and close together.

3 After the last wrap, clip off the end of the wrapping wire with the wire cutters, cutting in as close as possible.

4 Use the snipe nose pliers to smooth the end of the cut wire back against the wraps. You have made a single closed loop.

5 To form a closed loop above beads, place the round nose pliers against the bead to create a space similar in size to that filled by the wraps by your first closed loop. Bend the wire towards you at an angle of 90 degrees, making sure you don't lose the space marked by the pliers.

6 Change the angle of the round nose pliers so they are almost vertical to the beads. Roll the wire over the pliers to create another loop above the space.

7 Hold this loop in the snipe nose pliers and wrap the loose wire back towards the bead with your finger and thumb. Try to match the size of the original closed loop.

8 Clip off the excess wire and smooth in the end as you did in Steps 3 and 4.

Wiring to hang

This technique is an extension of the closed loop. Use it when you want a button to lie flat when suspended on a chain or thread.

Materials and tools

12cm (4³/₄in) 0.6mm silver-
plated wire
two-hole button
round nose pliers
snipe nose pliers
wire cutters

1 Thread the wire through a hole in the button that you want to hang. Fold the wire about 4cm (1½in) along.

2 Wrap the shorter end of the wire around the longer length several times with your finger and thumb, then finish the loop as you did in Steps 3 and 4 of making a closed loop.

3 Add a bead above these wraps and make another closed loop following the method shown in making a closed loop on pages 123–4. This loop should be sideways on to your hanging piece so adjust the angle of the pliers before you begin. Make sure your loop is large enough for your chosen thong or chain to pass through.

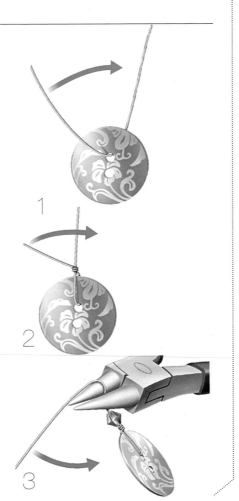

These stylish cufflinks are made by simply sewing pewter buttons onto cufflink findings with a strong thread. Use the thread double and sew the button onto the end of the chain in exactly the same way as you would sew a button onto clothing.

Crimping

This technique is used to attach a fastener to a necklace or a bracelet, or to group sections of buttons or beads onto a thread. To secure small groups of buttons or beads, work a French crimp onto the thread and squeeze it into position with crimping pliers using the bottom part of the pliers. Crimping pliers are specially designed for the task, but you can use snipe nose pliers or even round nose pliers, if you wish.

For almost instant earrings, glue pretty buttons with flat backs onto clip-on findings. Use strong glue and let dry for a couple of hours before wearing your earrings.

Materials and tools
T-bar fastener
French crimps
crimping pliers

1 To attach a fastener, position a French crimp on the thread. Slide the thread through one end of the fastener, then back through the crimp.

2 Place the crimp close enough to the fastener to make a neat loop, but not too close to prevent movement between strands of buttons or beads. Squeeze the crimp flat with the pliers, then clip off any excess thread.

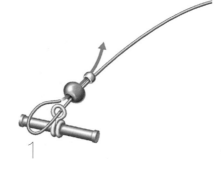

Overhand knot

This is what most of us think of as a simple knot. Make a loop in your thread or threads, pass one end through the loop and draw it tight. Overhand knots can be used decoratively and to hold small groups of buttons or beads in place.

Half knot

This is a spiralling knot that can be used to create a decorative finish to a necklace. You will need a one or more core threads and at least two 'working threads'.

---

1 Move the left thread under the core threads and over the right thread, but don't pull it tight.

2 Take the right thread over the core thread and under the left thread so that it passes through the loop made with the left thread and the core threads.

3 Pull the threads a little to tighten the half knot, then repeat the process. Once you have completed four or five knots you should see that the knotted shapes are forming an attractive spiral shape.

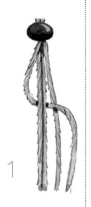

1

2

3

1

2

3

Square knot

This is a progression from the half knot and uses two different movements to create a flat knot. Again it is a good way to finish a necklace. You will need the same number of core and working threads as before.

---

1 Move the left thread under the core threads and over the right thread. Then move the right thread over the core threads and under the left thread so that it passes through the loop made with the left thread and the core threads.

2 Now reverse the movement: put the left thread over the core threads and under the right thread.

3 Move the right thread under the core threads and over the left thread. Keep alternating these movements until you have the required length.

Index

This index gives page references to the projects and techniques found in the book. Page numbers in *italics* refer to illustrations. As many of the same techniques are used throughout the book, the page references are intended to direct the reader to substantial entries only.

Credits

Breslich and Foss Ltd would like to thank the following individuals for their help in the production of this book: Sara Withers for writing the text and creating all the jewellery; Lindsey Stock for photographing the finished pieces and Martin Norris for the model shots; Kuo Kang Chen for his illustrations (knots by Kate Simunek); Michelle Pickering for editing the text; Tashi Archdale for modelling the jewellery; Jackie Jones for hair and make-up; Elizabeth Healey for designing the book.

It is with great sadness that we report the death of the very talented Lindsey Stock during the production of this book.

PERTH & KINROSS LIBRARIES